A Cat on Stage Left

An Alice Nestleton Mystery

Lydia Adamson

A SIGNET BOOK

SIGNET
Published by the Penguin Group
Penguin Putnam Inc., 375 Hudson Street,
New York, New York 10014, U.S.A.
Penguin Books Ltd, 27 Wrights Lane, London W8 5TZ, England
Penguin Books Australia Ltd, Ringwood, Victoria, Australia
Penguin Books Canada Ltd, 10 Alcorn Avenue,
Toronto, Ontario, Canada M4V 3B2
Penguin Books (N.Z.) Ltd, 182–190 Wairau Road,
Auckland 10, New Zealand

Penguin Books Ltd, Registered Offices:
Harmondsworth, Middlesex, England

Published by Signet, an imprint of Dutton NAL,
a member of Penguin Putnam Inc.
Previously published in a Dutton edition.

First Signet Printing, February, 1999
10 9 8 7 6 5 4 3 2

Chapter 1

It was one of those late-August afternoons in the city where everything becomes absolutely still except for the heat, which seems to move in noisy waves.

I was seated on a window ledge looking out over the street. Not a soul on the street. Bushy sat beside me, also staring down. Pancho was investigating the food dishes, particularly the one with his dry pebbles. He scorned them but kept returning to the dish again and again, as if he was investigating why he loathed them so much. My Pancho might be quite mad, but he is at heart an old gray intellectual.

Tony was fast asleep in my bed, having executed his usual behavior patterns: He showed up late last night, straight from a job at a summer theater near Cape May. We made love. Then I fed him. Then I went to sleep. He stayed up all night pacing. When I got up in the morning, he went to sleep, and he's been sleeping since.

The overhead fan was working fine, but nothing

could cut through the heat. I sat and watched and sweated. What I was watching for I don't know.

Then the phone rang. I picked it up at the first ring, not wanting to wake Tony.

It was a woman's voice. "Are you Alice Nestleton the cat-sitter?"

I began to laugh. It seemed to be such a strange question. *Are you Alice Nestleton the cat-sitter?*

I mean, why not, "Are you Alice Nestleton the actress?"

Or Alice Nestleton the gingersnap cookie addict?

Or Alice Nestleton, of *the* Minnesota Nestletons?

Or Alice Nestleton, the lady with the strange paranoid cat with only half a tail who loves saffron rice?

Then I recovered. I said, "Yes, I am. Who is this?"

"My name is Mary Singer," the caller said.

She had a husky, jumpy voice. She stopped talking after identifying herself, as if waiting for some kind of recognition from me.

But I didn't know her at all.

"Pernell Jacobs recommended you," she said in explanation.

Now *that* name rang a bell, but for the moment I couldn't remember why. Then I did remember and I blurted out, "But I haven't seen Pernell Jacobs in more than ten years."

In fact, it was closer to fifteen years. Pernell Jacobs had been in Tony Basillio's and my acting classes at the old Dramatic Workshop on 52nd Street in the 1970s. I might have bumped into him once or twice since then—in the early or mid-1980s. Pernell was a very handsome black man and a damn good actor. But he was a bit flaky, as they say.

"I haven't been in touch with Pernell in years," I told the caller. "How could he know I do cat-sitting these days?"

The caller didn't seem at all fazed by that question. She simply chose not to answer it.

Of course, there were any number of ways Pernell might have found out that I care for kitties between roles now. It could have simply been a matter of his running into an old colleague of ours who had more current information on my life.

"Will you take care of Dante for me?" she asked.

"Is that your cat?"

"Yes. He's big and sometimes a bit playful."

"Well, Mary," I said, "anything short of a Bengal tiger is acceptable. How long will you be away?"

"About four days."

"Starting when?"

"Starting now. When can I bring Dante over?"

"Oh, no. Just a minute. You don't bring the cat to me. I don't board cats. I'll come to your apartment while you're away and take care of him."

"That's not possible. Why can't you keep Dante with you?"

"Look. I told you. I don't run a boarding kennel. Why don't you just look in the Yellow Pages? You'll find one quick enough."

Mary Singer didn't respond. I waited. I hoped she would hang up forthwith.

Then I heard some garbled words.

"What? I can't hear you."

She said loud and clear: "I will pay you twenty-five hundred dollars to board Dante for four days."

"Twenty-five hundred!" I was incredulous.

"In cash. Up front. Just four days."

I didn't know how to respond. That was a lot of money to me at the time. A whole lot of money. But boarding? With Pancho and Bushy in the loft? Dangerous, very dangerous.

Again, she took my silence as an affirmation.

"I'll be in front of your apartment house in twenty minutes with Dante and the cash."

"It's not an apartment house. It's an old warehouse converted to lofts."

She hung up.

I looked around, growing increasingly frantic. What had I done?

What did I know about Dante? Nothing. Was he neutered? Was he hostile? How did I know there wouldn't be a battle royal? The only thing worse than a dog fight is a cat fight, because the kitties tend to hurt each other very quickly once they really engage.

Call her back, Alice, I told myself. Forget the twenty-five hundred. But I hadn't gotten her phone number. Was she in the phone book? Maybe. Maybe not.

I calmed down a bit. Tony was beginning to talk in his sleep.

What about a barrier? There were no doors in my loft except for the bathroom and the closets—and I surely couldn't keep Dante in one of those spaces for four days. But if I had some planks of wood, I could improvise a closed cat run in the loft.

If . . . if . . . if . . .

Pancho made a dash toward the bed but at the last moment veered off.

Bushy, my Maine coon cat, ambled under the beat-up dining room table and started to preen and groom himself. He was quite vain.

Then the solution came to me, right out of the air, as they say.

I simply would not take Dante out of his carrier. Tony would transport him immediately to his apartment—which used to be my apartment—and keep him there for four days, bringing him back to my loft just before Mary Singer arrived home to claim him. True, Tony had cats of his own now—two Siamese. But Tiny and Tim, as they were called, were so kind and sweet, you could put a hound dog in the room with them and not have to worry.

It was a wonderful solution. Everyone would be happy—with the possible exceptions of Tony and Dante. As for Tony, I'd give him half the twenty-five hundred to decrease his sadness. And as for Dante—well, maybe whole sardines and sweet cream and a lovely velvet mouse and some special organic cat grass and tea parties with the world's finest catnip.

Yes. It was a wonderful plan. I smiled as I watched Anthony Basillio sleep. Lover and friend and colleague. In what order? Should I wake him now and tell him, or wait until Dante was outside the loft in his carrier? I decided to postpone notification.

Then I walked out of the loft and downstairs to pick up the package.

The street was baking in the sun, but there was a surprisingly strong hot breeze whipping about. I leaned against the building.

Nobody was out—not even the dog walkers. Even the two winos from the east corner, who were permanent fixtures on the block, had sought shade and relief elsewhere.

I closed my eyes. Upstairs the heat was terrible. On the street, for some reason, it was bearable.

A car turned the corner and very slowly came down the street.

It was an astonishing vehicle. A wine-red Bentley with whitewall tires and all the chrome on it shined to a fare-thee-well. Was it chrome, or was it sterling silver?

I stepped toward the curb. I didn't know cars like this still existed except on movie lots.

The car stopped. And out of the Bentley stepped a character even more unbelievable than the vehicle he was driving.

This was the dream chauffeur of all times. He was

dressed in a luxurious gray uniform, and he must have been absolutely broiling in the heat.

He wore tall brightly shined black laced boots. Yes, laced high.

I was fascinated by his cap—the old-fashioned crushed kind with a small visor.

To make matters more bizarre, he was actually wearing some kind of driving goggles.

I couldn't tell whether he was thirty or sixty, but he was in excellent physical shape: erect, broad-shouldered, flat-stomached.

"Are you Miss Nestleton?" he asked.

"I thought I was. But now I'm not sure," I replied.

He didn't get the humor. He said gruffly, "Good!"

Then he opened the rear door. I could see a man on the far side of the seat. Next to him, closer to me, was a woman. And on the seat beside her, a carrier. It was one of the largest cat carriers I have ever seen. Inside the carrier I could make out two doleful eyes.

The woman—she was wearing a washed-out red dress and her hair was curly black—started to climb out of the Bentley with her cat.

Suddenly the man who had been sitting next to her gave her a violent shove.

Woman and carrier came hurtling out. The edge of the carrier smacked me on the knee.

I fell down.

I found myself on all fours, the pavement biting into my palms, staring at the woman who had been thrown from the car.

She, also, was on all fours. Her face was very lined—like Lotte Lenya at the end of her career.

"Are you okay?" I asked.

She didn't answer.

"Are you Mary Singer?"

Again, no answer.

A shadow fell over me. I looked up. The chauffeur. He had something in his hand. He pressed it against the back of the woman's head.

I didn't realize the object was a gun until he pulled the trigger.

The woman fell forward. Her face hit the pavement hard.

The chauffeur climbed into the car. The Bentley purred off.

For some reason all I could think of was Dante—the cat in the carrier. Help the cat, I said to myself. Save the cat.

My hands fumbled with the clasps. Wildly. My fingers were like trembling sticks. Finally I got the thing open and swung the top up.

Then I stared in disbelief at the large stuffed toy cat with painted buttons for eyes.

Chapter 2

After four hours of questioning by Detectives Warsaw and Gates at NYPD's Manhattan South headquarters, I was exhausted and still dazed from the shooting.

That's why I made a joke when a uniformed officer wheeled a TV set and VCR into the room where I was being questioned.

I said, "But I don't watch cop shows."

They didn't think it was funny.

Detective Gates started the tape.

"You didn't know you were about to become a TV star, did you, Miss Nestleton?" Warsaw asked, a bit nastily.

I didn't have the slightest idea what he was talking about until I saw that infernal Bentley suddenly materialize on the screen.

And then I saw the whole thing unfold again, on video.

Gates froze the frame with me on all fours opening the cat carrier, the dead woman right beside me.

I just sat there—rigid, silent, confused.

"A Canadian tourist named Hal Estes was standing on your corner with a video camera. He was intrigued by the Bentley. It seems he's an antique car buff. He got the Bentley on video. He followed it around the corner. He shot the murder. Then he sold the tape to the networks. You'll be on the evening news, Miss Nestleton. I don't know what he got paid for this stuff. He sold it in two hours. But whatever he got, you should get a piece of the action."

Warsaw's voice was no longer nasty. It was almost compassionate, in fact. He stood fiddling with the middle button on the Hawaiian-style shirt he was wearing.

Gates, the younger detective, shut the machine off. He said to me: "Mary Singer was her real name. Three of her neighbors from Spring Street just ID'd the body. But it took them a while. It seems they hadn't seen her for at least six months. And the last time they saw her she was fat. She'd lost a ton of weight. She went from a fat woman to a thin woman. At least, that's what they said. Are you sure you never spoke to Mary Singer before that phone call? Or met her? Maybe you have the same confusion. After all, if the lady lost all those pounds in that short a time, you might—"

"I'm sure," I interrupted with finality.

"We got the Bentley plate number from the tourist's video. Stolen plate. As for the car itself, only one

Bentley dealer left in the five boroughs. He doesn't have a clue." Warsaw's voice was now sad.

"You've been helpful, Miss Nestleton," said Gates. "I'm sorry we had to keep you so long. But one more thing before you go. Are you sure there is nothing else you can tell us about this Pernell Jacobs?"

"No. I told you everything. I haven't seen him in a long time."

"None of Mary Singer's neighbors seem to remember a black man fitting his description hanging around her."

"Talk to them again," I said. "They're probably in shock from looking at the body. Anyway, I don't care what her neighbors remember. She knew him. She told me so. She said he had recommended me."

"You know," Gates said gently, "she didn't have a cat."

"Yes. You already told me that."

We stared at each other. The air conditioning was not working well. Gates had a modish bow tie on and a short-sleeved white shirt with a coffee stain near the collar. Not only was he younger than Warsaw; he was taller and thinner. He kept moving about the room. Float like a butterfly, sting like a bee, I thought.

"Can we drive you home?" Warsaw offered.

"I'll walk."

When I got home there was a reception committee. Tony had called my friend Nora Karroll, who owns a bistro in the theater district, and my niece Alison, who lives with healthy, kindly, older Felix only two blocks away from my place. In fact, Felix owns the building I live in. He gave me the loft rent-free as a birthday present when I was a bit, as they say, down and out.

They were all there, I suppose, to cheer me up or to comfort me. But they all looked about as stunned as I must have.

They were about to be a whole lot more stunned. I flipped on the TV to the evening news.

The Canadian tourist was interviewed first. Then they ran his video. Again and again.

I picked Bushy up and held him in my lap and watched . . . and kept watching.

After five showings Felix decided it was time to inject some humor into the situation.

"Actually, Alice, you look quite lovely on video. Sort of like a cross between Glenn Close and Rita Hayworth."

"I agree," Tony said. "You should be in one of those cop series, as a wise lady DA."

"She doesn't look that old," said Nora.

I ignored them and hugged Bushy.

When it started getting dark, they all left—everyone except Tony, that is.

"Why don't you put me up one more night?" he asked.

"As you wish."

"Can I get you some food, Alice? You have to eat something."

"I'm not hungry."

"Okay. What do I do with the toy?"

"What toy?"

He pointed to one of the large windows. Oh my! It was the cat carrier, pushed against the wall between windows.

"What is that doing here?"

"I just brought it upstairs with me after you went to the police station. I don't even know why. It was just there, in the street. The cops didn't seem interested. I guess they thought it was yours. You were hugging it when I came downstairs. You were calling it Dante."

I stared at the object.

"Anyway, look, Alice, I'm going to get some sandwiches. You may not be hungry, but I am starved. I'll bring you back something for later."

He walked out of the loft. I let Bushy down, got off the chair, and walked to the carrier. I opened the lid, pulled the stuffed cat out, and set it down on the floor. It was even larger than I had thought.

Bushy and Pancho came over to investigate. They sniffed and wandered off.

It was, I also realized, a beautifully wrought object. The cat fur was lustrous and tawny. The button eyes were mother-of-pearl, flecked with yellow paint. The lynxlike ears were braided and carefully dyed.

And for the first time I realized that the feet were set on small rollers.

I pulled the cat. It rolled a bit.

For the first time that day I laughed.

I pulled again. It rolled further. Pancho zoomed by. Uh-oh! He was getting crazy.

I picked the rolling fake cat up and took it back to the carrier.

Suddenly my hands felt something on the fake animal's belly. I turned it over. A thick piece of paper was heavily Scotch-taped to the fur there.

I pulled off the tape and inspected the paper. Inside were twenty hundred-dollar bills and five fifties.

My fee? It had to be. But why had poor Mary Singer taped the money there?

And what was I supposed to do with it now?

I closed the carrier and walked back to my chair. The video images—not the event itself—kept flashing in my memory.

Above all, I saw those moments before the trigger was pulled, when Mary and I were both on all fours, staring at each other.

I closed my eyes tight, but I could not erase her lined face. I saw it with great clarity. Like a road map of inexplicable death. I began to cry. The bills fluttered out of my hand onto the floor.

When I awoke the next morning I saw several strange sights.

The first was my clock, which read 9:06. I never sleep that late.

The second sight was stranger still. Tony was seated on one of the window ledges, looking down onto the street. And on the ledge next to him, calm as could be, were my two cats, also staring down. Now, Bushy and Pancho never fight, but they never fraternize, either. And this, beyond all doubt, was an exercise in fraternization.

I sat up, saying nothing but continuing to watch the trio. All three seemed totally absorbed.

"What is going on?" I finally asked in a hushed voice. Why did I whisper like that? I don't know. There was just something so strange about the way they were all sitting there . . . together . . . gravely.

Tony turned toward me. He was smiling mysteriously. "You have become a shrine, Alice Nestleton."

"What are you talking about?"

"Come over here. Take a look."

I got out of bed, slipped on my robe, and walked over to the window. The gallery made room for me.

"Did you feed them?" I asked Tony just before I looked down.

"Of course."

Then I gazed down at the street, normally deserted during morning hours except for a few trucks that invariably got lost on their way to and from the nearby Holland Tunnel.

But now it was busy down there. People and cars.

Two young women were placing a bouquet of flowers where Mary Singer had been murdered.

Several other people were taking shots of my building with their cameras.

A large video camera was set up across the street and manned by two men who looked like professionals.

"Fools!" I shouted, so suddenly and savagely that Pancho and Bushy fled their seats.

I turned away from the window with a groan. "I want them away from here," I said.

"What are you going to do? It's a free country, Swede."

"I warned you not to call me that anymore."

"Calm down."

"I will not! I don't want to 'calm down.' "

I spotted the carrier with the toy cat then. I walked briskly over to it and kicked the damned thing. It survived the blow. My toes stung something awful. I had forgotten that I was wearing slippers.

"I don't want to stay here with *that* going on, Tony."

"It'll quiet down in a day or two," he replied.

I walked back to my bed and sat down. Mary Singer's $2500 was on the small table—the bills held together now by a thick red rubber band.

I was on the edge of a full-blown panic attack.

"Are you okay?" Tony asked. He was now standing between the window and the bed.

"No, I'm not okay."

"You want some coffee?"

"No."

He sat at the edge of the bed.

"Believe me, those idiots will all be gone in a couple of days."

"I don't even know if we can call them idiots," I said angrily. "They are leaving flowers."

"Just take it easy, Alice. You're starting to sound

out of control. Get dressed. We'll go for a walk and I'll buy you breakfast."

Breakfast. Yes. I realized then that I was ravenously hungry. The last food I had had was almost thirty-six hours ago. I threw on some clothes and we literally ran out of the building, past the startled sightseers.

We headed for our usual coffee shop. But when I saw a coffee wagon on Hudson Street, I stopped and ordered a large coffee and two jelly donuts.

"I've known you a long time, Madam Nestleton," Tony said. "I've known you in good times and bad. But this is the first time in living memory that I ever saw you buy a jelly donut. Are you really going to eat those?"

"Watch me."

We sat down on a stoop. I wolfed down the first donut and then immediately attacked number two. Then I felt nauseous. Tony handed me a napkin. He opened my container of coffee and watched while I drank it. I felt better after that. He went back to the cart and got me another container. I ate the last of the second donut. Tony started on his buttered roll.

It was a blessedly cool morning: the first intimation of autumn. People were walking briskly along Hudson, going to work. The heat, everyone knew, would return, but today was today. Seize the day. Walk the autumn walk.

"We're like kids, sitting on stoops," Tony mused.

"Better than crawling around on the sidewalk on all fours," I said bitterly.

Tony laughed.

"What do you find so funny?"

He held up his hands in a defensive, apologetic gesture. "Sorry."

"All right," I said. He leaned over and kissed me.

"Tony," I said quietly, "I'd like to get away for a few days."

"Where to?"

"Anywhere. I just want to get out of that loft for a while . . . away from the block . . . from the neighborhood."

"Stay with me."

"No."

"Then Nora. Or your niece. She and Felix have forty spare rooms."

I shook my head. "No. I just want to be alone, Tony. This thing has got to me. Bad. Will you watch over Bushy and Pancho?"

"Sure I will."

And that is how I ended up in Chinatown.

I'll explain: there is only one Holiday Inn in downtown Manhattan. It's on Lafayette Street, just north of Canal Street, on the fringes of Chinatown. There was a special rate of $119 per night.

Why that hotel?

I don't know.

Why check in with two canvas book bags instead of my usual small valise?

I don't know the answer to that one, either.

The room was furnished in Middle American gothic, which was fine by me.

I lay on the huge bed with the light off in the afternoon and the air conditioner on low. No audible street sounds at all.

Yes, I thought. This was what I needed . . . a brief respite from images—video and real life.

I dozed. I walked downstairs and had a bowl of soup in a Vietnamese restaurant. I came back to my room and read a few short stories by Saki. I called my agent at four o'clock. She had seen the video on the news, but she made no comment about it and how it might catapult my moribund acting career out of the muck and into the majors. I called Tony and Nora and Alison and assured them all I was fine.

That first night in the hotel I slept straight through from nine in the evening to seven in the morning. Then I dressed and went down to the lobby. The hotel was only about fifteen blocks from my loft, but it could have been another planet. Except for a few bewildered tourists, most of the guests seemed to be Hong Kong Chinese.

I ate a Chinese breakfast up the block on Lafayette Street: two delicate little buns and a cup of coffee. A rice and milk porridge tempted me—but I abstained.

When I got back to my room the chambermaid had already cleaned up.

I sat down on the bed. Everything was much better. That rock crushing my neck and head seemed to be rolling away.

And the images were softer. Maybe one more day, I thought, and I'll go back to the loft with Bushy and Pancho. My poor little friends. But I knew Tony was spoiling them beyond their wildest dreams. A-dollar-a-can cat food. Duck. Salmon. Halibut. No dry food or pebbles. Probably some saffron rice for Pancho. God knows what for Bushy. Maybe turkey tetrazzini. Oh yes. I was feeling much better. The dead are dead. I was simply at the wrong place at the wrong time. That's all. And so was that Canadian tourist with his ridiculous video camera.

In fact, I was feeling so much better that I went on a shopping expedition deep into Chinatown. I found an exotic herbs store and bought exquisite soaps for virtually everyone I knew. The store, with its amazing scents, made me drunk. I wandered around like Blanche Dubois. Now that was a role I had auditioned for at least a dozen times over a twenty-year period. But my Southern accent was so preposterous that I never got the part, even in an amateur production.

When I got back to the hotel with my ginseng and peach blossom and ylang-ylang treasures, all of them gift-wrapped, there was a message from Basillio to call him at my loft.

"What's up, Tony?" I asked as soon as he picked up.

"Something strange."

"More trouble?"

"Not really," he said. "I came up here to pick up your mail like you asked me to. So I bring the stuff upstairs, check everything out, and then go down to go home. As I'm turning the corner, this old derelict grabs my arm. At least I think he's an old derelict—you know, asking for wine money. I shake him off and say I have nothing to give him. Then he says, 'Are you a friend of Alice Nestleton's?' I say yes. He says he's a neighbor of Mary Singer and he has to talk to you. Now. Then he gives me a piece of paper with his name and number on it. I go upstairs again and call you."

"Give me the name and number."

"Sam Tully," Tony said, spelling it out, then reading the phone number to me.

"I'll be back at home tonight."

"You're cured?"

"I guess so. See you later."

I hung up then and began to dial Sam Tully's number. Was it some kind of scam? Could be, I realized. I put the phone down. I located the phone book. There was an S. Tully listed on Spring Street. Mary Singer had lived on Spring. The story checked out in that respect, though I didn't know the exact address of her building. I cross-checked. Mary Singer was not listed at all.

I dialed Tully's number again, this time letting it ring—three times.

Someone picked up. "Yeah?" Gravel voice.

"Is this Sam Tully?"

"Who wants to know?"

"My name is Alice Nestleton."

Pause. Then: "I don't want to talk on the phone. I'll be waiting for you tomorrow morning at eleven in a coffee shop called Heaven's Gate, on 25th Street just west of 3rd Avenue. I'll wait just fifteen minutes, honey, then I'm gone."

"My name is Alice, not Honey. And if you live on Spring, why not meet around there?"

"Take it or leave it."

"Look! What's this all about?"

He hung up. I didn't know what to make of him. But right then I had other things to do—like get ready to check out and go home.

Two hours later I was back in my loft with my kitties. They didn't seem ecstatic at being rescued from Tony. I accused them of selling me out for a few lousy cans of gourmet cat food. They neither confirmed nor denied the charge. But I still hugged them almost to death.

For some reason, I felt like I had been away a long time and those horrible events on the pavement outside my building had happened at some time in the dim past.

And my instinct was to forget all about the planned meeting with that Sam Tully. But, as my grandmother once told an irate neighbor, "Alice may appear to be a bit weird, but deep down she's a young lady."

And ladies, young or otherwise, always keep appointments.

Chapter 3

I've lived in Manhattan many, many years, but I never knew that a place like Heaven's Gate existed north of 14th Street or west of Avenue C. This was not a basement somewhere in the bowels of the East Village; this was slightly stuffy, high-rise-heavy Gramercy Park, and I used to live only three blocks away from this very spot.

I walked in, took one look, and halted in wonderment. Picture it: A simple room . . . not big, not small . . . filled with five stained and tattered sofas bleeding their stuffing, four easy chairs in similar condition, and three old-fashioned formica-top kitchen tables with dented straight-backed aluminum chairs. All placed randomly.

Here and there were standing ashtrays like you used to see in hotel lobbies.

There was an open tenement-style kitchen—a small fridge, a small range, cappuccino machines, and a long table for cutting and mincing and sandwich-making. Two great kitchen sinks that looked like washtubs completed the picture.

The background noise was folk rock music from a cassette player hanging on a hook on one wall.

An old schoolroom blackboard, hung on another wall, announced such daily specials as banana on five-grain bread, apricot iced tea, peanut butter and honey sandwich, and home-fried potatoes.

About fifteen children were milling about. And I do mean children. They appeared to range in age from fifteen to nineteen, but they had to be older, at least some of them. They were all smoking up a storm, all wearing earrings in peculiar places (noses, lips, and so on), and all dressed in that style borrowed from the cutting-edge black uptown kids and modified to downtown trendiness.

The truth was, they were all stunningly beautiful young people. Who were they? Where did they come from? I could only guess that they were students at the nearby School of Visual Arts or one of the City College campuses.

Several of them were speaking French, some German, some Hebrew. These were probably from the hostel-type hotel next door, which seemed to cater to the overseas backpack set.

Then I noticed the discordant element.

An old man was seated at one of the tables. The kids seemed to ignore him, and he was ignoring them. He was reading a newspaper. Or rather, he was faking reading the paper: his eyes were closed. He was napping, I could see when I got closer to him, with a cigarette dangling from the corner of his mouth.

This, I realized, had to be one Sam Tully.

Tony was right. The man looked like a derelict. In fact, the winos on my block looked a sight better than he.

Three-day white stubble on his face. Close-cropped gray hair that made his head look as if it had just been fumigated in some drunk tank. A jelly belly on a stout, collapsed frame. An ill-fitting gray T-shirt with the washed-out I ♥ NEW YORK logo across the chest.

On his feet were a pair of moccasins that might have been unearthed nineteenth-century artifacts.

There was an apparently untouched cup of coffee in front of him, a spoon sticking forlornly out of the liquid. Had he put it there and then fallen asleep before he could stir it?

I walked to the table and sat down on the seat directly across from him.

"Are you awake?" I asked sternly. The ash on his cigarette was very long. No wonder he wanted to meet me here, I thought. This was one of the few remaining coffee shops where smoking was permitted.

He opened his eyes.

"You Nestleton?"

"Yes."

"How's business?"

"I don't know what you mean."

"I mean the P.I. business."

"P.I.? Oh, you mean private investigator. No, you have it wrong. I'm not a private—I mean, a P.I."

He winked. "Sure, lady. Anything you say. Damn, you're a looker."

I guffawed at the outdated expression. "I believe, Mr. Tully, you're paying me a compliment. Thank you."

"Just call me Tully."

"As you wish."

He pulled the butt from his mouth. "Let's get down to business."

"Okay," I said. "What business is that, by the way?"

"Mary Singer told me about you a few years ago. She had read a piece in one of those local sheets about how an actress helped clean up a case for the NYPD. It had something to do with cats and murder. This actress, it seems, was also a cat-watcher."

"You mean cat-sitter."

"Whatever."

"I remember the article vaguely," I replied.

He sipped the coffee, almost poking his eye out with the spoon still in the cup. Then he leaned back and grinned.

"So do you get it, honey?"

"Get what?"

"She didn't show up at your place to board any cat. Mary didn't have a cat. She was about to hire you as a P.I."

"Did she tell you that?"

"No. She wasn't staying in her apartment. My place is right above hers. She wasn't around except to pick up the mail. I was collecting it from the box for her and putting it in her apartment. We would just run into each other briefly and she mentioned your name once."

"Look," I told him, "I don't know why Mary Singer called me. I don't know why she gave me that cock-and-bull story about boarding her cat. Or why she showed up with the fake cat in a carrier. Or who drove her to my place and murdered her. Or why."

"Get smart, Nestleton. I'm telling you what was going down."

"I don't understand what you're saying, Mr. Tully. What is your point?" The old buffoon was beginning to irritate me.

"She needed your help."

"Fine. She needed my help. For what?"

"Don't know." He lit another cigarette. "Yeah, you sure are a looker," he repeated.

"What did Mary Singer do for a living?" I asked.

"Retired accountant. She had plenty of bread. Nice lady. Weight problem, though. Always trying to get skinny. I guess it was a struggle for her, but that never stopped Mary."

"Stopped her from what?"

"You know—guys."

"Were you one of her guys, Mr. Tully?"

"Tully. Just Tully. I hate that 'mister' garbage. No,

I wasn't one of them. Boy, she had a real wild thing going with one fella. A few years ago. He was a doctor. Name of Hugo Rodman. It got messy. They sent him to the joint."

"What for?"

"Don't know."

"Have you told the police?"

"Tell the cops? Me? You must be kidding. Hey, listen, I don't think you realize who I am."

I didn't know how to respond, so I said nothing.

"You ever hear of Harry Bondo?"

"The name isn't familiar."

"Ever hear of a book called *Only the Dead Wear Socks*?"

"No."

"Hell. What's the point of even talking to you, then? Look. Harry Bondo was the toughest and smartest private eye ever to step out of the pages of a cheap paperback. And I invented him. And my third book in the Bondo series—*Only the Dead Wear Socks*—well, it's still considered one of the best by those in the know. Hell, one critic said Sam Tully makes Raymond Chandler look like Gore Vidal."

"I see. So you write detective stories."

"I don't write anything anymore. I'm just laying out my credentials for you, Nestleton. One pro to another."

"Look, Mr. Tul—Tully, that is. I am not a private detective and I don't write. And I don't know what you want me to do . . . about Mary Singer or anything else."

He grinned and winked at me once more. Then he walked out without saying another word.

I wondered whether I should get one of the apricot iced teas.

As I was wondering, Sam Tully walked back in. He didn't sit down again, though.

"I got the feeling, honey, that you don't trust me. Let me put you straight. I'm a good guy. I got a heart as big as a baby's posterior. Remember!"

He paused and jabbed an arthritic thumb in the air.

"Remember!" he repeated. "I've been taking care of Pickles for almost a year now."

"Who is Pickles?" I asked.

"Mary's leopard."

What on earth was this character talking about? A leopard? A leopard named Pickles?!

It couldn't be a real leopard he was talking about. They're illegal in Manhattan apartments. It couldn't be any kind of cat at all. Both the police officer and Tully himself had confirmed that Mary didn't have a cat.

I was so confused that all I could do was make a feeble joke. "Mary's leopard? I thought Mary had a little lamb."

"Not funny!" Sam Tully pronounced. And walked out.

When I got back to my loft I called the detective squad at Manhattan South. Detective Warsaw answered the phone. He listened quietly while I reported what I'd learned from Tully concerning Mary Singer's lover.

"Yeah," he replied when I had finished, "Dr. Hugo Rodman. We are aware of him. However, he died shortly after being released from prison for the illegal sale of amphetamine prescriptions. And that was a few years back." Warsaw laughed. "At this time Dr. Rodman is not a suspect in the case."

"Oh. Well, I just thought you would want the information. But I see you already have it."

"Yes, yes, Miss Nestleton. We appreciate your concern." He paused there. I could tell he was putting a piece of gum or hard candy into his mouth. I heard the unmistakable crinkle of paper.

"Have anything else for us?" he added.

"No."

"That's too bad. It's funny, Miss Nestleton, but it seems to be the consensus around here that you have a lot more to tell us."

"I'm sure I don't know what you're talking about, Detective."

"No? Well, it just seems strange to me . . . to everyone taking a look at this case, in fact."

My anger was building. I was becoming a bit frightened as well. I didn't even know why. But I managed to keep my voice level as I asked, "What is strange?"

"You gave us a meticulous description of the car and the uniformed driver with his goggles. Very clear, very detailed. The videotape which came to light confirmed that your descriptions were very accurate—right on the money. But the videotape couldn't see inside the vehicle. Only you could do that. And you did. Isn't that right, Miss Nestleton?"

"Yes."

"You saw a man push Mary Singer out of the car . . . didn't you?"

"I did."

"Yes. But suddenly your meticulous observation skills failed you. You say you can't give us anything at all about the man in the backseat. Was he black or white? Young or old? Fat or thin? Wearing a tie? Wearing running shoes? In a Dracula outfit? What? Nothing."

"Listen to me, Detective Warsaw. That man was in the shadows. It was morning. The block is in shadow and sunlight. The car door was open only for a split second. Everything was happening at once. I wouldn't think I'd have to explain something like that to a professional like yourself."

My explanation did not persuade him of anything. I heard him chewing his blasted gum. Or maybe it was a candy with a soft center. A Tootsie Roll?

"Hey, what can I say, Miss Nestleton? Thanks again." He hung up gently, almost cryptically, as if the very hanging up were designed to frighten me.

As for me, I slammed the receiver down hard. Who were they kidding? Did they really believe I could identify the man in the backseat and was withholding that information from them? For what reason would I do such a thing? Why?

I stormed around the loft for a few minutes. Maybe they thought the man in the back seat was the actor Pernell Jacobs, whom I had mentioned to them. It was Pernell who had told Mary Singer about me. Or so she said. But I had not seen him in years. And I had never known him very well. If it had been him in that car, I would have said so. Maybe it was him. I simply had no clear recollection of who was there— just that it was a male.

Then, for some reason or another, I had the sudden urge to look at that old article about me, which, according to Mr. Sam Tully, had caught the attention of Mary Singer.

I went to the Alice Nestleton archives, which now consists of two ratty post office mailers stuffed into a red laundry bag.

One contained birth certificate, divorce papers from first and only marriage, and assorted legal documents asserting I was alive and who I claimed to be.

The other envelope contained clippings . . . long ones from when I was a child prodigy at the Guthrie Theater in Minneapolis . . . and a great many shorter notices in appreciation of me as the finest perpetually out-of-work actress ever to grace Off Broadway. And there were a few others lambasting or extolling individual performances, including the infamous one written in response to my Cleopatra in an avant-garde production of the Bard's play. "This interpretation of Cleopatra," the New York critic had written, "is the most demented one I have ever seen. Ms. Nestleton seems to think the woman was a borderline psychotic with nymphomaniacal tendencies."

But I was looking for a different kind of notice. I quickly located the yellowing item, cut from a free neighborhood weekly.

The headline read: CAT WOMAN TO THE RESCUE.

There was a definite tongue-in-cheek cast to the writing: a neighborhood resident, Miss Alice Nestleton, a cat-sitter, had, according to the precinct captain, provided invaluable help to New York homicide detectives in solving a grisly double murder. The article went on to hint that I was some kind of psychic.

An obviously idiotic take on me and the part I had played in events.

Whatever I thought about the piece, this had to be the one Tully was talking about. It even had a photo of me acting in a Dürrenmatt play whose title escapes me.

Yes, this was the article that had intrigued Mary Singer. But so what?

I began to stuff all the clippings back into the mailer. But then I heard a strange noise: a kind of repeating *ping*.

Was it the pipes? That was all I needed right then—a damn flood in the loft.

No. It wasn't the pipes and it wasn't the cats playing with their dry food. Someone was pelting one of the large windows from outside with rocks or something.

My first thought was that some of the sightseers had returned to their macabre shrine and wanted me to pose for their cameras. Maybe they wanted to get snaps of me wheeling Dante around.

I rushed angrily to the window, flung it wide open, and leaned out to get a better view of the street.

But there were no sightseers down there, no cameras. The only one on the street below was Tony Basillio. His arm was raised to throw more loose gravel at the window.

"What are you doing?" I shouted down at him.

Tony lowered his throwing arm down and smiled shyly.

Then he began to emote: "But soft! what light through yonder window breaks? It is the east, and Juliet is the sun!"

It was obvious he was drunk.

"Come up here, Tony!" I pushed the window back down, but not all the way.

I stood by the apartment door and waited for him. I could hear him struggling up the steps, singing snatches of "Surabaya-Johnny."

He couldn't make the last three steps.

"I'm dizzy," he said, holding onto the rail.

His face was a pale green. I took him by the arm, helped him into the apartment, led him over to the bed, and plopped him down. Then I went after a washcloth, wet it, and wiped his face and neck. He was sweating bullets.

"You can't drink in hot weather, Basillio. When will you learn that? After you're in the grave?"

Tony held up three fingers.

"What does that mean?" I asked.

"Three. Just . . . three. That's all I had."

"Three what, you silly man?"

"Bandies. I mean, brandies."

"That's two and nine-tenths too many."

He took the cloth out of my hands. "I've got to talk to you," he said anxiously.

"Talk."

He leaned back on the bed, resting on his elbows. He was breathing heavily, in and out, with great effort. Tony Basillio, I realized, was beginning to look his age. His face, still handsome, was thickening.

"I feel better now." He nodded a few times. "Much better. Sit down next to me."

I did as he asked. Nearby, Bushy was watching me closely.

"Do you remember that pet store on 23rd Street?" Tony asked.

"I think so. You mean the one east of 3rd Avenue?"

"Yes. That one. It has this huge rabbit in the front window, in a cage. The rabbit is so big he fills the cage completely. There's little room for him to walk about. But oddly enough, the rabbit always looks very happy . . . contented. He just looks out and twitches his huge rabbit nose. I say hello to him every morning. This morning I walked past and he was gone. The cage was gone. Had someone bought him? Did he die? I didn't know. I wanted to go inside the store and simply ask, but I was afraid to. Don't ask me why. The whole thing made me very depressed. I went for a long walk. Then I went into a bar on 3rd Avenue and had a brandy. I'm the only one in the place except for the bartender. He's a big man—huge. I get the funny fantasy that he'll change into a huge rabbit and his nose will start to twitch at me."

Tony stopped talking and stared at the washcloth in his hands as if trying to understand how it got there.

"I don't understand the point of your story, Tony. . . . Is there a point?"

"I'm getting to it. It has nothing to do with rabbits. See, there's a television in the bar. There was a soccer game on some weird channel. Then that French news program comes on. You know the one I mean? It has English subtitles. It's broadcast first over in France and then a day later it comes on here. And wouldn't you know it!"

"Know what?" I asked, growing impatient with this saga.

"They're playing that video—your video—with the murder outside your place. Alice Nestleton's greatest role, played down on all fours. Next, they interview the tourist who made the video with his ugly little camera. I watch. How many times have I seen that same tape and that same interview? Ten times at least. But right there, at the bar, after my second brandy, I realize . . . I realize for the first time . . ."

"Realize what?"

"That I know him. I know the guy with the video camera. Oh, he's aged a lot and his hair is combed different. But I know him."

"You're drunk, Basillio. Where would you know him from? That man is a tourist from Canada."

"So he claims. So he says. So the world believes."

"All right, then who is he?"

"His name, Swede, is Flip Mariah. And he's in the business. He's a New York actor."

"Are you sure of that?"

"Very sure. I used to bump into him all the time— at parties, just around. He was on the fringes of that avant-garde company The Living Theater."

I couldn't believe what I was hearing.

"What do I do?" Tony asked. "Tell the cops?"

"No," I said, without really knowing why—at first. But the rationale came to me very quickly. Something strange was going on. Old names and old faces of the New York theater world were beginning to sur- face. Not just surface—they were in pursuit. And I seemed to be the one they were chasing.

"No, no police, Tony," I repeated. "Not now. Not yet."

"Then what?"

I took his hand in mine and held it tight. Menace seemed to have invaded my loft. I looked across the room. Who had taken that ridiculous toy out of the carrier? Me?

Chapter 4

We were seated in Nora's small cluttered office in the back of her restaurant, Pal Joey Bistro. It was early evening. Not even the pre-theater diners were there yet. The kitchen was silent. Three or four of the regulars were seated at the bar.

Yes, the brain trust had been assembled—Tony, Nora, and myself. The door of the office was left slightly ajar to admit some of the colder air from the main area of the bistro, which was air-conditioned.

I had laid out in clear, concise terms for Nora what Tony had discovered about the so-called tourist.

And for both Nora and Tony what I had learned from Mary Singer's neighbor Sam Tully.

"But that's not all," I said. "The NYPD thinks I'm lying to them."

"About what?" Nora asked, incredulous. Or maybe she was tweaking me a little. I have been known to be slightly less than forthcoming with the authorities.

"They think I could, if I wanted to, give them a

description of the man in the backseat with Mary Singer. The one who threw her out of the car."

"You know cops," Tony said wearily.

I gave him a quick and dirty look.

"So I have the feeling," I continued, "that the old man Sam Tully was right. Mary Singer was seeking me out for something other than a cat-boarding adventure. And I have the strange sinking feeling in the pit of my stomach that I—or rather we—all three of us—are somehow implicated in her death. Not directly, of course, but in some way we have yet to discover."

"That's insane, Alice," replied Nora angrily.

"Fantasy," Tony echoed.

"I'm not saying we pulled the trigger or guided the gun. I mean that all these names from the past are suddenly appearing. Out of nowhere. Isn't that true? And don't you find it at all strange? Mary Singer said Pernell Jacobs recommended me. We all went to acting classes with him—right? Tony recognizes this phony tourist as an actor he used to know in the golden days. Not a real friend of ours, but someone from our circle—one of 'our people,' as Tony likes to say."

I stopped there, suddenly disheartened. There was a long, awkward silence. Nora looked tired and a little downhearted, too. She had cut her thick red hair very short for the summer. Her face looked plumper. The vivacity of the song-and-dance gal, which was what she was, and which made her such a wonderful hoofer—like Mary Martin—had been drained away by the long summer.

"What are you really saying?" Tony asked.

"Look, Tony, what I'm *really* saying is, it's about time we all started making inquiries. Look up old friends and check out old haunts. Find out who those characters are and where they have been all these years. People like Pernell Jacobs and Flip Mariah."

"Old friends?" There was a bittersweet edge to Nora's voice.

"Yes, that's right."

Tony reached over and patted her hand. "Don't you understand, Nora? When Alice starts talking about making 'inquiries,' it means she doesn't know what the hell she's doing."

That was a low blow. Tony could be nasty sometimes. Nora ignored him, though. There was a sad, troubled look about her. "Alice," she said patiently, "you exaggerate how many of us there are left. Believe me, most of those old friends you talk about are long gone—gone from the theater and gone from New York. They went back home to have babies and get jobs and . . . well, you know . . . all the rest of it. 'Regular' lives, as some people might call it."

"Not all of them, Nora," I said stubbornly. "Now, I can't force you and Tony to get your butts in gear, but as for me—I'm going to find Joseph Grablewski."

Tony's eyes widened. "You must be kidding!"

"Grablewski . . . Grablewski," Nora repeated the

name perplexedly. "Now where did I hear that name before?"

Basillio laughed. "You mean you don't remember the resident genius at the Dramatic Workshop when we were all there? He taught drama theory, history, and directing, along with several acting classes. Alice used to chase after him, panting like a lovestruck puppy. But he never gave her a tumble."

I went red.

"As much as I hate to admit it," I said, "Tony is right. Grablewski thought I was just another stupid little hopeful from the cornfield. He used to whistle the Miss America theme when I asked him a question. He was a difficult man."

"He's got to be dead by now, Swede," said Tony. "He was a serious, take-no-prisoners alcoholic, in case you've forgotten. They don't live to a ripe old age."

"Maybe. Maybe not."

"When was the last time you saw him?"

"Five, six years ago. In—well, in a bar, on West 44th. I needed some information about old members of Stanislavski's theater group in Moscow who had emigrated to the States. I was looking into the murder of a young man, a student of mine. He was in a class I was teaching at the New School."

"Yeah," snapped Tony, "and if I recall, Grablewski was too stoned to tell you much of anything."

"Your memory is full of holes, Tony," I snapped right back. "He told me just what I needed to know. Even drunk, Joseph Grablewski knows more about the theater than any five sober people. He can tell you who directed what and where fifteen years ago—or fifty years ago—even if the production opened and closed in three nights and was mounted in an attic in Brooklyn."

I sat back, going over in my mind that strange meeting I had had with him. Thinking about it gave me a chill. Grablewski had been so bitter, so unforgiving. Yes, he had answered my questions. But he had cursed the whole concept of Broadway and mocked my craft. He had written his obituary of American theater in his blood alcohol level. Was he still alive? Sane? Findable? Approachable?

Plates were beginning to clank in the kitchen.

"Well?" I asked, looking at my companions. "What's it going to be? Can I count on you to make some calls?"

Nora shrugged. "Sure."

"Oh, those days of wine and roses," Tony muttered.

But then he leaned toward me and whispered amorously, "I will leave no stone unturned . . . no cafe unvisited . . . no nubile young actress uninterrogated . . . for your love, Swede."

"How nice you are—for a stage designer," I replied mockingly.

The meeting was adjourned.

It took me the better part of the next day to locate Joseph Grablewski. The shabby bar on West 44th

Street was, miraculously, still there, but the bartender said he hadn't seen Joe in a long time. Two years ago Grablewski had passed out in the bar and was rushed to St. Clare's Hospital with internal bleeding. It was rumored that he had survived and gone upstate to take "the cure."

He never showed up in the bar again.

The bartender, however, did not speak of Grablewski with distaste. He seemed to be aware that Joseph had once been something special, that people had sought him out even when he was sprawled blind drunk in one of the booths.

Just as I was walking out, he gave me the name of a priest who knew Joseph. This Father Cecci could be found at the St. John the Baptist parish on West 38th Street when he wasn't prowling the West Side bars looking for lost souls.

I found the priest easily enough. He was screwing in a lightbulb in the vestry of the church.

"What do you want Joseph for?" he asked, a bit suspicious.

I steadied the chair he was standing on. "I'm an old student of his, from the Dramatic Workshop."

"I see. He's doing fine—*and* he's sober. But I haven't seen him in a while."

Father Cecci gave me the name of one Lowell Boyne. He could be found in a shoe store on 8th Avenue. He was, the priest said, a friend of Joseph's—an old actor. Maybe he knew where to find Joe.

Boyne wasn't very hard to locate, either. But he sent me to someone else. And that old acquaintance of Grablewski's sent me to someone else. I was beginning to feel like a hand-me-down snowsuit. They all knew Joseph Grablewski. But none of them knew exactly where he was right now.

Finally, one man who worked in a record store on Broadway said that I'd probably find Joe "in Bookers."

I was astonished. Joseph Grablewski in Bookers? It didn't make sense. Bookers was a coffee shop on West 43rd famous as a gathering place for bit players and out-of-work actors; for has-beens and never-weres; for the theatrical lame, halt, and blind.

They all sat there for hours drinking coffee and reading *Backstage* or *Variety* and telling each other stories about the parts they almost had, the greats they had known and loved and hated.

Some people thought Bookers colorful. Some went there to hear theatrical gossip—no matter how outlandish, unreliable, or just plain untrue. Others called it sad.

An intellectual like Joseph Grablewski in Bookers was difficult to believe.

Did I have any other option, though? No. After all, it wasn't the first time I'd been there.

I once had a boyfriend who used to take me there with a hidden tape recorder. He wanted to collect the authentic laments of authentic theater people.

Poor fool. All he had to do was talk a little more to me.

The moment I walked in and saw that nothing had changed except for an ugly new paint job, I felt nostalgic.

I purchased a mug of coffee at the counter—there were no cups in Bookers—and threaded my way between the tables. It was crowded, as usual, and the many intense low conversations created a carpet of buzz, punctuated occasionally by a raucous laugh.

I got halfway through the aisle and there he was. Or was he?

I was confused, unsure. I took two steps forward.

Yes, it was Grablewski. But how he had changed!

He was well groomed and sat erect and alone at his table. He appeared to be absorbed in whatever it was he was writing in a spiral notebook. A stack of closed spiral notebooks lay next to his arm. His shock of white hair was brushed back. He looked, if anything, younger than when we'd last met—like a prematurely gray man of forty. But of course he was closer to seventy than forty. Joseph had put on weight, making him seem more solid, less ethereal. The hawklike face had lost its ferocity. It was almost kindly now.

I walked quietly over to his table and waited a long moment before speaking.

"Joseph?"

He did not respond.

I repeated his name.

He never looked up from his notebook.

"Joseph Grablewski . . . damn you . . . look at me!"

He stopped writing then, but still did not look up. I took the empty chair next to him.

Finally, and ever so slowly, he looked at me, with what seemed to be extreme wariness.

"I'm Alice Nestleton. I took your classes at the Dramatic Workshop. And I talked to you about five years ago. It was in that bar on—"

"How nice to see you again," he interrupted gently.

It was a gross understatement to say he had changed. Where was the sardonic bite? Where the witty barbs, the bitter put-downs? Just "how nice to see you again." It took me a moment to recover. I had primed myself for a battle.

"What are you writing?" I asked.

"A play."

"The last time I saw you, your view was that the American theater in general and Broadway in particular were utterly corrupt. Irredeemable. Hopeless."

"I'm sober now," he said. "Nothing is hopeless. And redemption is not something I think about anymore. Just day-by-day words. Like 'pen,' 'coffee,' 'sunlight,' 'heat,' 'cold.' Simple words. 'Redemption' and words like it are out of my vocabulary."

He began to play with his pen. I thought I could read uneasiness in the gesture and in his facial expressions.

I picked up my coffee with both hands, sipped,

and placed the mug back down. Why hadn't I thought to order iced coffee?

"I need your help again," I said.

He picked at the knot in his tie, and it wasn't until that moment that I noticed he was overdressed for summer—a gabardine suit, yellow shirt, and black tie. "Did you say I helped you then—five years ago?"

"Very much. You gave me information about actors who had once worked with Stanislavski."

"I don't remember. But I'll try to be of help again."

At last his hands came to rest. He lay his ballpoint pen down, fastidiously, on the open page of the notebook. I could see that he wrote in a tiny print style.

"I need information on two actors. One of them is named Pernell Jacobs."

He blinked a couple of times and repeated the name slowly, almost with affection. It was obviously a name from the past associated with good memories rather than travail.

"You know him?"

Grablewski sat back and stared past me. "I think," he finally said, "the last time I saw him perform was in 1982. It was, if I recall correctly, an all-black production of *Coriolanus*, done by a small company, in the tradition of the Negro Ensemble Company. It closed in two weeks. Pernell was quite good. In fact, he was one of the best natural actors I ever saw. But he had major flaws. He didn't know how to prepare a role, for one thing. And he never learned how to pace himself. He acted as though he were a hand grenade—just pulling the pin and exploding."

"And since that performance?"

"Nothing. I never saw him onstage again after that. I don't remember hearing about him again."

"All right," I said. "What about Flip Mariah?"

"Who?"

"Mariah. Flip Mariah."

"I don't think so . . . no, wait. Now that I think, it is familiar. He was a downtown actor with a couple of different experimental groups. Like those people on Wooster Street. Yes. I do recall hearing of one production. Maybe 1984 or '85. I don't remember the title exactly. Gringo Something. Or Something Gringo—was it *Sweet Gringo*? Or perhaps *Sweaty Gringo*? It was a play with music, I'm fairly sure. Very cabaret. Very sleazy. And very erotic."

"Nothing else on either of them?"

"Not really."

"I mean about where they are now or what they're doing."

He shook his head. "No. I've told you what I know." Joseph cocked his head then. "Why are you interested in those two?"

"I need to contact them. It's just—well, it has to do with a personal debt that has to be repaid."

"Debt!" he repeated, laughing, though I had no idea why. "Whose debt?"

"Does the name Mary Singer ring a bell?"

"No. Who is that—an actress?"

"I don't know. I don't think so," I replied.

He shrugged. I could tell he was anxious to get back to his writing; he wanted me to leave. I wasn't quite ready to go, though.

"What's your play about?" I asked.

"Nothing," he replied, "absolutely nothing." And for the first time I caught a whiff of the old Grablewski sarcasm.

I stood then, thanked him profusely for his help, and started for the exit.

"Just a moment," he called out.

I stopped and looked back at him.

"How goes it with you?" he said.

"The struggle continues."

"Use it," he said. Ever the acting teacher.

When I got home from the Grablewski adventure I fed the cats and lay down for a nap.

It was early evening when Tony's call came in.

No, he had found nothing so far—"*except*," he began to stammer—"except for a kind of rumor . . . a kind of feeling among certain people."

"Give it up, Tony! What did you find?"

"Calm down. What's got you so on edge, Swede? It's just that a few people I talked to seemed to be hinting that Flip Mariah got into trouble several years ago."

"What kind of trouble?"

"Bad trouble."

"What does that mean?"

"I couldn't find out. But he's an actor, right? So it had to be drugs, whiskey, women, or insanity."

"What a nice list."

"I thought you'd appreciate it."

Nora phoned twenty minutes later. She had made some calls, she said, and she had seen some people. "*Nada*," was her one-word report. But she couldn't stay on the phone a minute longer, she said. The bistro was jumping.

I made myself a cup of tea, shut off the overhead fan, which had been rattling noisily for the past few hours, and opened all the windows wide.

Then I sat down on the floor—about the best place to sit in summer—and stared at Dante, the big toy cat on wheels.

Obviously I was a bit disheartened. Grablewski hadn't told me much. Tony had merely dug up an old slander—perhaps true, perhaps not.

And Nora had drawn a complete blank. In fact, she didn't seem interested in helping me at all.

"You are a stupid-looking feline," I told Dante. "No character, no subtlety about you. A fake cat is not supposed to look fake. And you do. At least Mary had lines on her face."

I was caught short by my own insensitivity toward the dead woman.

But then again, it was those Lotte Lenya lines on Mary Singer's face that were burned into my memory.

Where had all those lines come from? How had

she earned them? Mary Singer had not been so old. According to Sam Tully, she had had a lover: a doctor. He apparently hadn't considered her too old. Then it occurred to me: weight loss. Often when mature people drop a great deal of weight quickly, they wrinkle that way; they seem to shrink away from their skin. Isn't that what the fitness nuts were always going on about—toning, firming?

Bushy had wandered over and was rubbing his back against my knee. My old boy was getting plump. Maybe, I thought, I'll take him to the vet and ask for one of those newfangled "natural" diets for him: collard greens and salmon roe, or something like that.

I laughed out loud. It spooked Bushy.

But it must have been that burst of laughter that enlightened me.

No matter the cause, I had the sudden realization that whatever the relationship between Mary Singer and Dr. Hugo Rodman—it had to be something more than a romance.

Of course! The good doctor had been convicted of prescribing speed illegally. And speed was *the* diet drug. Obesity had to have been one of his specialties. And fat Mary Singer had gone to him for help with her weight problem. There must have been records of her treatment.

I was working myself up to a fever pitch. Even though he was dead, the records might still be available—from an associate of the doctor, maybe. Or from his wife. From someone. There had to be a case history on Mary Singer somewhere.

The police must have realized this. They had checked out that relationship very quickly. But they seemed to have found nothing out of the ordinary. Maybe they weren't looking for the right thing in the right place.

I rushed to the phone and called Tully.

"Yeah, what is it, honey?" he said after I identified myself.

I let him get away with the "honey" this time. It was the smart thing to do. Because a few seconds later he told me that Rodman was indeed survived by a widow. He gave me her name and where she could be found.

I slept on the floor that night.

Chapter 5

It was one of those odd, small stores that make Lexington Avenue in the area north of 79th Street so distinctive. Half book store, half gift shop, with the single theme being cooking.

Cora Rodman was dusting expensive saucepans when I entered. She was wearing a peasant dress with a low neckline. Her brown hair was cut short. She might have been my age, or even a bit younger.

She wore fishermen's sandals without socks. Her toenails were painted a dull red. She was stout—not fat—and very curvaceous.

I was intrigued by her dusting technique. She manipulated the cloth so lightly, as if she were sending raindrops onto the object. As if she were dispensing rather than gathering.

The store had obviously just opened for the day. I was the only customer.

She started when she noticed me standing just inside the door. Then she pointed at me with the hand holding the dust cloth. "I know you!" she announced emphatically.

"Really? I don't think we've ever met."

"Oh, I know you. I surely have seen your face before." And she gave out a kind of theatrical gasp and brought her hands to the sides of her face. "My God, you're the poor woman crawling around crazily on the sidewalk in that video!"

Oh. That. I'd forgotten about that.

Whatever cover I had was already blown. But I hadn't really intended to lie about my identity.

"You're right," I said. "That is me in the video, crawling around crazily, like you said. My name is Alice Nestleton."

She had one more compassion-filled look for me. But then her face hardened.

"If this has anything to do with Mary Singer," the widow said, "I would suggest you turn around and walk right out of my store."

It was not what I had expected. I began to fumfer. "Perhaps I'm just here to buy a cookbook on Afghan cuisine."

I got a scornful look from her. But it gave me time to recover. "The woman is dead, you know. She deserves some justice."

Cora Rodman laughed. "Some would argue that a bitch deserves nothing."

"Oh? Is that what she was?"

"The quintessential tramp," she said, folding her dust rag as if it were a precious linen napkin.

"I'm aware that Mary Singer was your husband's—that she had an affair with Dr. Rodman."

"And what else are you aware of?"

It was no time to play coy. "Of the fact that he was sent to prison for the illegal prescribing of amphetamines."

"He did nothing wrong. Nothing."

"All right, Mrs. Rodman. If you say so. I'm not here to argue the rights and wrongs of your husband's conviction."

"What are you here for, Miss Nestleton? Flowers for Mary Singer's grave? A contribution?"

"Her medical records."

"Her what?"

"I believe she was Dr. Rodman's patient as well as his lover."

"How do you know that?"

"Logic. Yes, it's a logical inference. An informed guess. After all, he treated obesity, didn't he? And Mary had that problem."

"I knew very little about my husband's practice. And I know absolutely nothing about that woman's physical condition."

"What happened to his case files?"

"I don't know and I don't care."

"Did you ever meet Mary Singer personally?"

"We passed each other in the hall."

"Hall?"

"The hall of mirrors."

"What are you talking about, Mrs. Rodman?"

"Nothing. Nonsense. I'm talking nonsense to you, Miss Otis. Just as you're talking it to me."

"My name isn't Otis. It's Nestleton."

"Good. Let me give it to you straight. I'm sorry when anybody's murdered. I'm sorry you were forced to witness it. But I hated Mary Singer. I blame her and all the rest of my husband's patients, lovers, friends, professional associates, spiritual gurus, and financial advisors for the terrible things that happened to him. He was a profoundly naive man. Innocent in the best and most real sense of the word. Do you know what I'm saying? Raw meat for ravenous homewreckers."

"And you, Mrs. Rodman. Is there any blame to be placed on your shoulders?"

"Go away."

"Just tell me where I can find his files. They must be somewhere. Just let me look at them for fifteen minutes."

"Go away now."

So I walked out of the store. But once outside I stood rooted to the sidewalk. That woman inside, I realized, would never disclose anything of substance—if indeed she knew anything. She was beyond redemption.

I looked uptown and downtown and I experienced, if you'll pardon the expression, a strange case of dèjá vu.

I was maybe ten years old. It was a warm Minnesota day, at dusk. I was near the barn door and I saw my grandmother standing halfway between the dairy barn and the house.

She was standing quite still and looking out over her property and beyond—to the thick woods on the north and the hilly green slopes to the west and south.

There was something very strange about the way she looked. As if what she was seeing was a form of desolation.

But it wasn't. The view was fertile and beautiful.

I remember the disquiet I felt, just watching her, knowing something was quite wrong but not being able to name it. Knowing it had to do with some kind of desolation.

But of course as a child I didn't know that word—*desolation*. I learned it years later, and yet I still hardly know its full meaning.

Believe me, I felt it that morning outside Cora Rodman's shop. As my grandmother must have felt it.

I began walking slowly downtown. The lines in poor Mary Singer's face were becoming etched in my consciousness.

Alas, being old enough to have been trained as a Method actress when the Method was still vital, I knew what an acting teacher would say. It's a prop.

It was later that day—about three in the afternoon—when I swung into Pal Joey in the theater district and made my way straight back to Nora's private office. I had picked up Dante at my loft and brought him along in his carrier.

The moment she saw me and my package, she cried out in horror. "Why did you bring that thing in here, Alice? It spooks the hell out of me."

"Relax. It's in the carrier," I said, gently placing Dante on the floor.

"It looks like some kind of voodoo doll," Nora muttered.

"I never thought of that," I admitted. "Anyway, Tony will be here in a few minutes."

"Oh? What for?"

"To illuminate the current situation. To plan the next step. To . . ."

"Want a cold drink, Alice?"

"Vodka and tonic would be good."

She climbed out from behind her desk, shouted the order out to the bar area, and sat back down. The three drinks came in a jiffy. I took mine, Nora took hers, and we left Tony's on the desk.

"I'll be with you in a minute," Nora said, "body and soul."

I could see she was writing checks. And occasionally punching furiously at a small calculator.

"What's that you're doing?" I asked, sipping the bracing drink through a straw.

"Figuring the 2/10 EOM."

"What?"

"Let's say I'm buying paper napkins and drinking straws from a wholesaler. I buy a few dozen of each. Then I get sent a bill about the twentieth of the month. If I pay the bill before the tenth of the following month, I can take two percent off the total. 'EOM' stands for end of month. The other thing, 'two-ten,' stands for two percent/ten days. Get it?''

I nodded. She went back to her checkbook. The overhead fan sucked in the air-conditioned blasts from the dining area. It made me drowsy. The drink had lost its allure. I looked up at the fan's blades, moving much more slowly than one would think they should. Nora started to sing snatches of some show tune as she worked.

"He's late," I noted, to no one in particular.

"He always is," Nora replied, aborting the song, slamming the checkbook shut, flinging the calculator into a desk drawer, and attacking her drink.

Tony arrived thirty-five minutes later.

"You'll never guess what happened to me."

"You were hit by a truck," Nora offered.

"Maybe next time, Nora," Tony said. "No, what happened was, I was walking uptown on 7th Avenue and suddenly I heard snatches of music in my head."

He began to hum something neither Nora nor I recognized.

"Then," he continued, "the words of a song just popped into my head along with the music. So I started singing. And then I realized I had actually composed the words and music of a brilliant piece called 'The Stage Designer Blues.' And ladies, it's dynamite."

Nora burst into hearty laughter.

"Do you want me to do the whole song for you?" he said.

"Later, Tony," I said. With Tony Basillio it was hard to tell when he was serious and when he was not. Maybe "Stage Designer Blues" existed. Maybe not. But who cared?

"I think I am becoming whimsical in my old age," he speculated.

"It's those two crazy Siamese cats you live with now, Tony," Nora cautioned. "They would make anyone whimsical. But be careful—hear? After whimsy comes confusion."

"And then desolation," I added grimly.

"Desolation? What the hell is the matter with you, Alice? What desolation?" Nora threw up her hands in disgust and repeated, with the same emotion: "Desolation!"

Tony kissed me. "My desolation angel," he purred.

"Let's get on with business now," I said.

"What business?" he asked, puzzled.

"Mary Singer, of course."

A silence descended and I caught a quick, nervous exchange of glances between Tony and Nora. I didn't know what to make of it. In fact, it rattled me.

"What?" I demanded. "What's going on with you two? Is this some kind of conspiracy the two of you are brewing up?"

"Not really," answered Tony.

"Then what?"

"It was just that when you brought up that name again—the warning lights began to flash."

"Exactly," said Nora in agreement.

I looked from one to the other of them, saying nothing.

"Alice," Nora said sternly, "leave this one alone."

"You mean Mary Singer's death?"

"Yes."

"Why?"

"I . . . I don't know exactly. But you didn't come out of the mess of her death too well, you know. You need to distance yourself from it."

"I see. You mean you think I'm still in shock from the murder? You both think I don't know what the hell I'm doing. Is that it?"

"Something like that," Tony mumbled.

"You just listen to me, both of you. I need your help—now. But if you're not happy about giving it, just say so . . . and I'll go elsewhere."

Again, silence.

"Well," I pressed, "is it yes or no?"

They each gave me a reluctant nod.

"Okay, then, like I said, let's get to it. Nora, I have a research project for you."

"Sure," she said tonelessly.

"Find a link between Pernell Jacobs and Flip Mariah."

"How do you know there is one?"

"There *has* to be. Pernell recommended me to Mary Singer, she said. He told her I was a reliable cat-sitter. Although we know she probably knew about me for a long time—from an old clipping. But Mary must have known Pernell in some way, right? Then Flip Mariah videotaped her death. Maybe he did it to make a quick buck. Maybe it was all a huge coincidence and he was just walking by. Maybe he used a phony name for any one of a hundred reasons. Or maybe he and Mary were somehow conjoined. In some kind of relationship."

"What kind of relationship, though? What kind of link are you talking about, Alice?"

"Theatrical? Let's start with that first."

"You mean they could have worked in a show together—something like that?"

"Yes, that's just what I mean, Nora. Some kind of existing theatrical connection: acting, producing, directing . . . whatever."

"But I've already asked around about that sort of thing. I got nothing. And if that old drunken genius of yours—Grablewski—couldn't make a connection, then what chance do I have?"

"Let's just be thorough this time. No friends. No drunks. Just the historical record."

"Record? What are you talking about, Alice? What record?" Nora was shouting now.

Basillio was enjoying her frustration, all but clapping with glee. I gave him a nasty look, and he feigned contriteness.

"Nora," I said, turning back to her, "don't you remember those volumes called *Theater Annuals*?"

"Sure I do. With the year of record after each title. I was in the *Theater Annual* many times when I was working steadily. It was sort of a yearly roundup of all theatrical events: with casts, plots, photos, critical notices, and such. Sort of an expanded, intelligent, collated yearly *Playbill*. But those things haven't been published in years, Alice."

"She's right," Tony concurred. "I think they went out of business in the late eighties."

"So what?" I said impatiently. "It's a place to start. Get over to the Lincoln Center library, Nora."

"And tell me again what I'm looking for."

"Some connection between Pernell Jacobs and Flip Mariah."

"Maybe they just swam in the same pool somewhere."

"Fine. If that's what you find out, that's what you find out. After the annuals, check out old health club records. And anything else you can think of. Even if it's something . . . off the wall."

"You mean like racquetball?" Tony asked, deadpan.

"Very funny, Tony. I'm coming to your assignment right now."

He saluted me military-style. I picked up the pet carrier and put it on Nora's desk. Then I opened the top and pulled the insane-looking Dante out.

Holding the toy with both hands, I turned its head—glassy eyes and all—toward Tony.

He shrank away from Dante's glance. "Have mercy!"

"Take a good look, Tony."

"No thanks. I've had a conversation with him already. You seem to be forgetting that I was the one who rescued him from the street."

"No, I didn't forget." Then I thrust Dante into his arms.

"What do you want me to do—sing him to sleep?"

"Find out where he came from."

"How am I supposed to do that?"

"Hit all the toy stores."

"Aw, c'mon. They don't sell creatures like this in toy stores. He ain't exactly a cuddly little teddy bear."

"I don't mean places like Toys 'Я' Us, Tony. I mean high-priced chic places, like F.A.O. Schwarz, or some of those Madison Avenue places. Sure, Dante is strange. But who knows? There are a lot of strange stuffed animals around. Mary had to have bought it somewhere—or someone else purchased it for her."

He heaved a sigh. "Okay."

"And if you can't dig up anything by going the toy store route, break it down."

"Break it? You lost me there."

"Look at the eyes, Tony."

"I'm looking."

"What do you see?"

"Eyes."

"No. Not eyes. They're mother-of-pearl buttons. So check out button stores."

"Oh for God's sake, Swede. How do I know where to look for buttons?"

"Let your fingers do the walking—Yellow Pages. And check out his fur, too."

"And how do I do that?"

I grasped Tony's hand and ran it along Dante's back. "What do you feel, Tony?"

"Uh . . . fur?"

"What kind of fur?"

"I don't know."

"I think it's called mouton. There was a time when everybody's Aunt Eileen owned a mouton coat."

Nora reached over and stroked the material then. "I think you're right," she said.

"So?" asked Tony. "So it's mouton. So what?"

"So visit some of those remnant places in the fur district."

"You're kidding."

"I'm not. And in addition to that, here, look at Dante's feet."

"They're wheels. Like roller skates."

"Wooden wheels, Tony. Very old-fashioned. No one skates on wooden wheels anymore. They use high-tech plastics—Rollerblades. The only place you'll find roller skates with wheels like these nowadays is an antique store. You know, a place that would sell Americana—nostalgia."

"Kitsch," Nora said in explanation.

"I get the picture," Tony said, and then rammed Dante back into his carrier and slammed the lid shut.

The silence that settled over the room this time was an out-and-out pall. We all reached for our now-watery drinks. The fan blades seemed to be moving a bit faster now.

It was obvious that my friends were not happy with their assignments or with me. The longer I sat there, the more those facts depressed me. Finally, I made a feeble excuse and just walked out.

Nora called to me as I left: "Remember the Alamo!"

I had no idea what she meant by that. Lost causes? But then, Nora had a very weird sense of humor sometimes.

I began the long walk home. No longer oppressively hot, the weather had taken a sudden turn. The sky was threateningly dark, winds whipping at the summer skirts of the ladies. It felt like hurricane weather. But no rains fell.

I turned off Hudson Street. Only twenty yards away from home.

Then I saw the car. Parked right in front of my building. No, it wasn't the Bentley from hell. But it was large and dirty and menacing. I stopped short. There were two men inside. One of them spotted me in the rearview mirror and stuck his hand out the window to wave at me.

Then and only then I realized who the men were:

Detectives Warsaw and Gates in their unmarked police vehicle. I approached the car and looked inside.

Behind the wheel, Warsaw was eating an ice cream sandwich. Gates, the one who had noticed me in the mirror, was drinking from a can of A&W root beer.

"We've been waiting for you, Miss Nestleton," Gates said.

"I find that oddly charming," I replied.

"We're charming guys," Warsaw said. He was wearing a quiet sports shirt this time. He was eating his ice cream with precision—a bit from each side, diminishing it symmetrically.

"How was your day?" Gates asked.

"It's not over yet, obviously. I can't make a judgment."

Gates stared at his root beer can as if he were reading the label for potential impurities.

Warsaw finished his ice cream sandwich and crumpled the wrapper.

"You have anything to tell us?" he asked me, smiling.

For some reason the question infuriated me. I decided it was time to give them something to chew on besides empty calories.

"Yes," I said. "That Canadian tourist who made the video lied to you. He's really a New York actor named Flip Mariah."

I waited for the astonishment to register.

"Well," Gates said laconically, "everyone knows New York actors will do anything for a buck."

Warsaw got out of the car and spoke to me over the top of the hood. We must have looked like two ducks negotiating a stream.

"We don't care about the video, Miss Nestleton. We want to know who you saw in the back of that Bentley. We want to know who was seated beside Mary Singer in that vehicle—the man who pushed her out. Simple. Just tell us what you saw."

Gates exited the car next. He stood very close to me.

"The shock wears off," he said. "The memories come back. I think you have something to tell us now. It seems strange to me that a fine actress like yourself—and an upstanding citizen, which everyone says you are—would withhold information from the police. I think maybe you just didn't have any loose change for a call. But here we are. You don't even have to spend a quarter."

I didn't reply. I merely stared at his face . . . for a long time. Then at Warsaw's face. Both handsome men. Both fairly civil. They seemed to be good public servants. They were not harassing me in any manner; just seeking relevant data from an eyewitness in a murder investigation.

Yet I felt a distinct threat. I was actually frightened of them. I knew it was absurd—but there it was.

Without saying a word, I turned on my heel and walked quickly into the building.

Once inside, I lay down, feeling defeated and drained. I was asleep in seconds. Bushy and Pancho woke me twenty minutes or so later with their chorus of moans and yips. Feeding time. Depressed, defeated, frightened, whatever—I was expected to feed them.

Groggily, I spooned out their meals. Then I stood by and watched them eat. The rain had finally come, along with lightning and thunder. The flashes and claps seemed to clarify my situation. I had no confidence in Nora and Tony at this point. Why? I didn't know. I guess it was because their lack of enthusiasm for the case was so palpable. For that matter, I had little confidence in my own ability to proceed with the investigation. And as for the NYPD, they perceived me not only as an impediment but almost as a kind of noncriminal accessory.

But I knew very well that nothing in heaven nor on earth was going to stop me from bringing some kind of peace to Mary Singer.

I crawled back to bed and tried to continue my nap, but it was no good. I lay there listening to the rain. One thing was sure: I needed help badly, and would get nowhere without it. I could think of only one person to turn to: that magnificent sleuth Harry Bondo, who had uttered the immortal phrase that became a book title—*Only the Dead Wear Socks*.

In other words, it was time for me to throw in with Sam Tully.

Chapter 6

"So you finally stopped all this pussyfooting around and went with the money," Tully said, sipping his shot of bourbon.

Eleven in the morning was far too early for me to have a drink, but, at Tully's request, I had purchased one for him. We were in one of those perpetually dark bars south of Canal Street on West Broadway.

I just stared at him for a moment and then said, gently, "Two questions, Mr. Tully. Just two. One: what are you talking about? Two: how does a man your age drink that poison in the morning?"

"I'll answer the second question first, honey. Only old people can handle bourbon, see. We're already in hell. As for the other question, what I mean is, it's about time we got together, you and me, to clear up this mess. I'm your man. You take care of me and I'll take care of you. Catch my drift?"

"You have a strange way of speaking."

"Is that so?" He folded his arms.

"No insult intended. Maybe it's a regional dialect

peculiar to people who live on Spring Street between West Broadway and Sixth Avenue. But I don't remember Mary Singer speaking in that dialect over the phone."

"Her and me understood each other perfectly," Sam countered, finishing his drink with a flourish and actually smacking his lips.

"That's what I'm counting on. Yes. I propose we join forces."

"Smart move, honey."

"Do me a favor and don't call me honey anymore."

"Okay. What do I call you?"

"Alice."

"Naw. Don't like it."

"How about just Nestleton? Me Nestleton. You Tully."

"Not bad." He lifted a finger to signal to the bartender that he wanted another drink. He lit a cigarette and blew the smoke expansively upwards. God, the poor man was a wreck.

"Let's set some ground rules, Nestleton."

"Sure."

"I don't work without an expense account."

I choked back a laugh. "Wait a minute, Tully. I'm not hiring you. You're no more a P.I. than I am. This isn't a dime novel, it's real life. All I want is your help and advice. Besides, I don't have a dime."

"Oh," he said, "well then . . . forget it."

"What else?"

"Here's what else. I want to put something to you

kind of . . . delicate, Nestleton. Listen, you're a looker—and young—and we both know that you people—"

"Just a minute," I interrupted. "What do mean by 'you people'?"

"Kids."

"I'm no kid, Tully. I'm not that young."

"Well, here's what I'm trying to say: I know young ladies sort of have this thing for old guys. You know, daddy trouble. As I said, you're a looker, but I ain't interested. Nope."

I nearly fell off my bar stool. Lord! The old fool thought I wanted to seduce him. But all I said was, "You have my word that I will control my primeval urges."

Having reached agreement on the ground rules, we left the bar and walked to Spring Street.

"That's it!" he shouted, startling me. Sam was pointing at a very old, faded blue five-story building on the south side of Spring, a block or so east of 6th Avenue. There were stores on the ground floor.

I stared at the building.

"What are you grinning at, Nestleton?"

"I'm not grinning, I'm smiling. When I first came to New York I had a definite idea about where I wanted to live. It was in a place just like that. You know, an old walkup in Soho or the Village with crumbling pastel blue paint outside and wall-to-wall poets and actors and writers inside."

"Where did you come from?"

"Minnesota."

"It figures. Look, honey—I mean, Nestleton—there ain't no poets in this building. And the floors slope and the pipes work only three days a week. It may be Soho on a tourist map, but that's about all."

"All right. I get the point."

"You sure you want to go into her apartment?"

"Yes."

"The cops went over it with a fine-toothed comb."

"We're not cops."

"True."

"It makes sense to me."

"Maybe."

"You have the key, don't you?"

"Sure."

"Good. I want to get a flavor of the woman."

"Sure."

"You sound skeptical, Tully. What would the great Harry Bondo do in our situation?"

"Honey, he wouldn't be in our situation."

We went in, walked up three treacherously worn and rickety flights of stairs, and approached Mary Singer's apartment.

"Wait a minute, Nestleton. You want to say hello to Pickles first?"

I had forgotten all about that leopard fantasy of his.

"If you think it's appropriate," I replied.

"Sure. Let's go. But don't say anything about Mary. I haven't told Pickles the bad news yet. I mean,

Mary gave him to me over a year ago to look out for—because she wasn't around much. But Pickles still misses her."

So instead of going into Mary's apartment, we climbed another flight and entered Sam Tully's dwelling.

It was an old-fashioned railroad flat—one room after another in a straight line. The furniture was all dark wood, and splintering. Humongous dust balls hulked everywhere.

Sam led me into the kitchen.

"Sit down," he said.

The large window was wide open. I could see the fire escape.

Sam brought two glasses of tap water and sat next to me.

"Pickles will show up in a minute or so if I make some noise."

He banged one of the glasses on the table.

"Where is he now?" I asked.

"Up on the roof."

I didn't say anything. The whole thing was fantastic. A leopard on the roof, eh?

"Yeah," Tully continued. "He likes it up there. Pigeons and puddles. He likes to hunt birds, but he never gets any. And he likes to jump into puddles of rainwater."

Sam banged the glass again.

Then a face appeared in the window. And a body.

Then a beast sauntered from the fire escape into the kitchen.

I was too astonished to speak. Pickles was the size of an ordinary house cat, but he had the coat of a leopard: dark spots on a light yellow background.

"I call him Pickles because some of his spots look like gherkins."

The cat rubbed against me. I saw a clearly defined white spot on the back of each of his dark ears. They triggered a memory.

"Wait a minute!" I cried. "This is a Bengal cat."

"The hell it is. Bengal tigers have stripes, lady. Pickles don't have stripes, he's got spots. He's a midget leopard."

"No, no, Tully. Bengal is the name of a new breed of house cat. It isn't even recognized yet by all the cat associations."

I tried to remember everything I'd read about it. I tried to communicate the information to the skeptical Sam Tully.

"It comes from the small Asian Leopard cat," I said. "Something like the ocelot. Original home was India, Thailand . . . places like that. They crossed the wild stock with some Abyssinian, Burmese, and Egyptian Mau, I think. And they got a wonderful house cat, so I hear. Look at Pickles's ears. The white spots identify him as a Bengal cat, along with his coat and the fact that he likes water."

I picked the cat up and kissed him lightly on the nose. "You are my first Bengal ever," I told him.

Pickles looked a bit embarrassed at my sudden outpouring of affection.

"If he's a house cat," Tully said with a sneer, "I'm Georges Simenon."

"Why would I make this up, Tully? I'm telling you the truth! And would you mind telling me why you let a lovely little catty like Pickles roam all over the fire escape and roof? Don't you know how dangerous that is for him?"

"You know what you are, Nestleton? You're what they used to call a sob sister."

I clammed up, trying to control my anger. I took a sip of the tepid water.

Finally I announced, with much restraint, "I would like to see Mary's apartment now—if you don't mind."

We walked down one flight, and Tully let us in. The apartment had obviously been carved out of a larger one. It bore no structural relation to Sam's flat on the floor above.

I was surprised at the spareness of it.

"I don't understand," I said, turning to Sam. "The police didn't empty the place out, did they?"

"No," he said.

"But I thought she *lived* here."

"She did. But in the last few months she kept on getting rid of the furniture. Nice stuff she had, too. I mean, guys would show up with notes from Mary and they'd just pull the stuff out. Sometimes the super let them in. Sometimes I took care of it. She wasn't around too much the last few months, as I said. And when she did come by to pick up her mail and I'd ask her what the hell was going on, she'd just shrug. She had lost so much weight she was starting to look sick."

I surveyed the small three-room apartment. "I always thought these buildings would have very high ceilings."

"Wrong again."

The kitchen had a stove, a refrigerator, one big cabinet over the sink, and a folding step stool. There wasn't room for a table.

No windows in the kitchen, either. The range was spanking clean. The refrigerator was empty except for five lemons.

The living room contained a sofa along with a coffee table.

Nothing on the walls save her framed college and accounting degrees. "How long had Mary lived here?" I asked Sam.

"Not long. Maybe twenty years."

I smiled. "That's all?"

"Yeah. I remember when she moved in. I like fat people, see. I was happy to have her near."

It was strange how neutral and un-homey the apartment seemed. As if no one had ever really lived in it, or as if it were a modest little place someone kept tucked away for the rare night spent in town. True, Tully had just told me about the furniture being taken out of the place. But that didn't account for the feel of anonymity about the apartment. No, there was something more to it.

Tully accompanied me into the bedroom. There was a single bed with a sunflower quilt, a small desk with carefully stacked papers on it, and a large open closet with clothes and shoes neatly arranged. There was no chest of drawers; her underthings were folded on shelves built into the closet.

"The cops went through her papers," Tully told me. "Didn't find anything much, though. Just a couple of utility bills and the deed to some property. Mary owned some land in Vermont. They turned the closet inside out."

"Well, at least they put everything back neatly," I noted.

"Downtown bulls ain't bad," said Sam.

"What about photo albums or something like that?"

He shook his head. "The lady was pretty much alone in the world. I know I never heard her mention family. In fact, I never saw her have any visitors, either, except for the boyfriends who'd occasionally come to pick her up."

I sat down on the bed, facing the two large windows that looked out onto Spring Street through the fire escape.

I put my feet on the ugly little straw mat between the bed and the window. It was the kind of cheap object that usually served as a doormat outside the apartment door.

Tully sat down beside me.

"You know, Nestleton, it was a hit."

"I'm not following you, Tully."

"*Mary* was hit—whacked . . . executed."

"I'm aware of that."

"I mean, it was done in a way I never heard of before. Like—" He paused.

"Like what?"

"It's hard to put into words. Like it was a hit—and not a hit. It was fake—but it was real. It was like a movie. Damn! . . . Yeah, that's what I mean. Like some ridiculous war movie. That's what it was like."

"You mean it was a performance of some kind?"

"Right on the money."

I felt uncomfortable. His comments had brought to the surface something I really had not dealt with before. The fact that the whole bloody horror did indeed have a performative, almost choreographic aspect. It was confusing to me as well as to Tully. And it made the whole thing even more frightening.

Who were the actors? Who was the audience?

"Will you look at that!" I heard Tully exclaim.

"What?"

"The rug."

I looked down once more at the tatty rug.

"There's writing on it, and it ain't 'Welcome,' " Sam said.

Sure enough, on closer look, there was some sort

of writing on the mat. It was either stamped on or woven into the sisal.

"It looks like a foreign language," I said.

I dropped to my knees and sounded out the letters: "*Aut Caesar Aut Nihil.* That's Latin, isn't it?"

"Sounds like. It sure ain't English."

"Any idea what it means?"

"Beats me."

"Why would anyone put Latin on a cheap old doormat?"

"Don't know."

"Have you ever noticed it before?"

"No. I was never in her bedroom before."

I got up and took my seat on the bed again. I closed my eyes tightly, a headache coming on strong.

"Lucille would know," Tully said.

"Who's Lucille?"

"Lucille Petinos. She used to teach over at St. Anthony's, on Macdougal Street. Doesn't work anymore. Never figured out how she gets by."

We finished our futile search and locked up, then began the short walk over to Prince Street with the words from the mat transcribed onto a piece of paper.

Lucille Petinos did not greet us warmly. It seemed that she had no desire to see us at all—well, no desire to see Sam Tully, anyway; I didn't even know Miss Petinos.

Her apartment was filled with cut flowers—vases of them on every available surface. Asleep at her feet was a Chow dog. She offered us, not very graciously, walnuts and apples.

She and Sam made small talk about everything from the weather to old neighborhood residents to Chow puppies. I couldn't help noticing that Sam, despite Lucille's initial unfriendliness, seemed very happy to be in her presence. This woman was very soft-spoken, but she seemed to energize the old writer.

Finally he remembered why we were there. He took the slip of paper from me and thrust it toward her. "This is Latin, isn't it? We need a translation," he declared.

Lucille took the paper and glanced at it. I noticed for the first time that she was absurdly overdressed for the season. She was wearing a thick black crepe dress, a strange kind of mesh stockings, and heavy shoes with squat heels.

Maybe, I thought, she dresses in solidarity with her dog. Chows suffer in summertime unless they're shaved, and then they look like crazy rodeo clowns.

"It's just a saying—you know, an expression," Lucille said. "It means 'Either Caesar or nothing.' In other words, if I can't be Caesar I prefer to be dead. If I can't have a job at a million dollars a year, I won't work. If I can't be Shakespeare, I won't write. To put it another way, I'll gamble everything on a dream."

"All or nothing at all," I offered. "Like the song says."

"That's right," she confirmed.

Lucille handed the paper back to Tully. A promising clue seemed to have turned to ashes rather quickly.

"What is this about, Sam?" she asked.

"A neighbor of mine got whacked. She had this mat on the floor. Those words were written on it."

"What kind of mat?"

"You tell her," Sam said to me, plainly frustrated.

"It was in her bedroom," I said. "Just an ordinary kind of woven thing you might use outside the door to wipe your muddy feet on. Those words are either woven on or stamped on. We don't know why."

Lucille then made us the most delicious coffee. Soon afterwards, we left.

In the small park at the end of Prince Street we sat down on a stone bench. The cars on 6th Avenue zoomed by us.

"I have found, Sam, that when I don't know what to do or don't know what I'm doing, I will sometimes focus on an object or idea that has no relevance at all to the problem at hand. But out of frustration, I will begin to treat it as though it mattered tremendously. I'll inflate it until it takes on great importance."

"That's a mouthful, Nestleton."

"I'm talking about the mat."

"I figured you were."

"I'm going home to think."

"Good idea. I'll catch you later."

So Sam Tully limped south and I headed west.

There were three phone messages on the machine. One was from my last remaining credit card company, requesting my very late monthly payment. One was from someone trying to reach a Dr. Kravitz.

The third call was from Nora.

She was breathless with excitement. "Get here fast! Do I have news for you!"

I took a quick shower and ate on the run—a piece of mild New York State cheddar and a stale croissant.

A few minutes later I was out on Hudson Street hopping a cab uptown.

Isn't that a wonderful expression? Hopping a cab. I've always loved it and use it all the time, although I don't have the slightest idea about its origin. Something equine? Hop a pony, Alice. Something nautical? Hop a freighter to the South Seas, Alice, and become an outcast of the islands.

Anyway, I may have been hopping, but the cab wasn't. We became hopelessly mired in traffic at 8th Avenue and 26th Street.

It was hot, no air conditioning in the car. Heat rose in waves from the street like taffeta crinkling. All the windows were rolled down, and a small swivel fan on the dashboard, which was next to useless, sent the barest breeze into the backseat.

I shut my eyes and tried to tune out the noise of the blaring horns and shouting drivers.

In a minute my driver joined in the chorus. He

was Haitian and his shouts were tinged with a French accent. "It is him! It is him!"

Startled, I leaned forward. "What are you yelling about?"

"See him? And him? It's the trucks. They double-park. They are the criminal. Explode them!"

I sat back again. Yes, I thought I understood what he was saying. This traffic jam, my driver was speculating, was caused by double-parked trucks. And his recommendation was that they all be blown to bits.

At least he had a suspect for the crime.

I had none whatsoever. The cab began to move forward slowly. This thing with Mary Singer, I realized, was quite astonishing. There were no identifiable suspects. There was an anonymous shooter dressed in chauffeur's clothing and goggles. There was the man who pushed Mary out of the car to her doom, who could not be identified because an eyewitness—me—was incompetent. There was a New York actor who had videotaped the crime posing as a tourist, and who might be involved in the murder in some way. There was a mysterious black actor in the murky background, whose name had been mentioned by the murder victim.

No *suspects*. How do you solve a crime with no suspects? Create them?

I knew the police had one. Surely they suspected Cora Rodman. By her own admission, she hated Mary Singer. She blamed her for her doctor husband's demise. But I didn't think Cora Rodman had anything to do with Mary Singer's death. It was just a hunch, but a strong one.

The cab was moving more quickly now. We were on our way again.

If I really wanted to fabricate a suspect, I thought, it would have to be Sam Tully. After all, he had been Singer's neighbor of record—and maybe more.

And, as his co-conspirator, the woman Lucille Petinos and her Chow.

Motive? Maybe Mary Singer killed Harry Bondo. Oh, well, one gets crazy in the summer in cabs.

I gave the driver a very small tip and rushed into Pal Joey. Nora was seated at the bar preparing a list of specials for the evening.

When she saw me she looked startled. "Alice. What are you doing here?"

"Are you crazy? You left an urgent message on my machine, Nora. You told me to hurry right over."

She broke into a grin. It was obvious now that she had been ribbing me.

"I was at that library the minute it opened this morning, Alice. And you're not going to believe what I found in *Theater Annual* for 1985."

"Tell me."

"A production of Christopher Marlowe's *Edward the Second* done Off Broadway in May '85."

"And?"

"You're going to love this, Alice. Both Pernell Jacobs and Flip Mariah had roles."

"Bingo!" I shouted. So loudly the bartender stared at me.

"Don't mind her," Nora reassured her employee. "She's quite mad."

Then she said to me, "And that isn't all. Guess who the star was."

'I can't."

"Lara Streeter."

I remembered the name vaguely. Something terrible was attached to it. What?

"Don't you remember what happened? It was all over the papers for a day or so."

"No, I don't."

"She killed herself during the run. And the play closed down."

Now I remembered. It had been a sad thing indeed. The rumors were that Lara Streeter was a bulimic. Supposedly she had been depressed over her ballooning weight and inability to lose it faster. And she had been taking all kinds of diuretics and other pills.

"Well?" Nora demanded.

"You did a wonderful job," I said. But she had given me so many startling facts that I couldn't begin to make sense of them immediately. I needed to think.

One thing, however, was clear as crystal: Pernell Jacobs and Flip Mariah knew each other. They had a real connection, albeit a theatrical one.

"I have to think on all this, Nora," I said. "Let me have the stuff."

"Stuff?"

"The pages you xeroxed from the *Theater Annual*."

She reddened. "Oh. It never dawned on me to xerox them. I mean, I was so excited at what I found . . ."

"Damn, Nora! You know better than that. What's the matter with you? It would have taken all of thirty seconds."

"Well, excuse me, Missy! I thought I did pretty good."

I reined in my temper. "Yes, yes, of course you did. I'm sorry. I'll get over there and do it myself."

"How about one of my onion tarts to speed you on the way? They're spectacular today."

I kissed her on the cheek, rushed out, hopped another cab, and was at the library in Lincoln Center within ten minutes.

It took me twenty minutes to find the volume. I pulled it off the shelf, went to the desk for change, and then hurried to the copier.

But the damn pages on *Edward the Second* had been ripped out.

I was so astonished I had to sit down. The pages had obviously been removed between the time Nora consulted them and the time I arrived.

That meant someone was following Nora.

I cringed. Had I placed her in danger? Was Tony being watched, too? And me?

I looked around furtively for suspicious characters. There were many. But none of them appeared to be watching me.

Clearly the information in the annual was crucial. How much more of it was there?

I replaced the book on the periodical shelf and asked the librarian which other venues in Manhattan had a complete run of the now-defunct *Theater Annual*.

"Mid-Manhattan Library," she replied immediately.

Another cab. Destination: 40th and 5th. I was down to my last two bucks.

It took me about forty minutes to locate the bound volumes. What did it matter? The pages were missing from this one also. *Edward the Second* had vanished here and probably everywhere.

I telephoned Detective Warsaw from a pay phone in the library's lobby. I got Detective Gates. I told him that the actor who had recommended me as a cat-sitter to Mary Singer and the bogus Canadian tourist knew each other and had worked with each other in at least one show.

Gates replied, a bit sardonically, "We have photos of both those individuals. We have been unable to locate them. They have no known addresses at this time. Do you have anything else to tell us, Miss Nestleton?"

I hung up, took the subway home, and crawled into bed. I was exhausted.

Before I could drift off, the phone rang. It was my

agent. I let the machine take care of it. She just wanted to know how I was bearing up under the heat. She meant the weather.

A woman called from the Upper East Side. Could I watch her cat over Labor Day weekend? Again, I didn't bother to pick up.

Sam Tully called, too. His message said that Lucille Petinos had called him just to say that I was a "stunner." By the way, he was on the case with a few "new angles."

He also admitted that I might just be right about Pickles. The cat might not be a midget leopard after all.

Once again I tried to sleep. I tried to trick my body clock by changing into my pajamas. It worked for a while, but I was soon awake again, troubled by bad dreams.

I tumbled around on the bed with Bushy and his catnip mouse with the red tail. Gloomy Pancho looked on disapprovingly while we frolicked.

Around ten that evening I had a terrible salad for dinner, and sat at the table thinking I ought to rearrange the kitchen cabinets. At least, I ought to think about thinking about it. But then Tony showed up. Mad as hell.

As he stepped into the loft, Dante under one arm and the pet carrier under the other, he demanded, "Get me some kerosene and a box of matches!"

"What for?"

"To make toast out of Dante."

"Take it easy, Tony. I had a difficult day, too."

"Dear Alice, you don't know what the word *difficult* means. I went to twenty-nine toy stores—twenty-nine! Uptown and down. West Side and East Side. Walking, climbing, subway, bus, truck, and kayak. I've been to stores that sell G.I. Joe and stores that sell thousand-dollar stuffed platypuses. I smiled. I scraped. I bowed. I begged. No one ever saw, heard of, or sold anything like this beast.

"And then I hit the button stores. You don't know what misery is, Swede, until you've confronted an old lady with a pince-nez standing behind a button counter and looking at you holding a stuffed feline on roller skates with mother-of-pearl eyes. Oh, you really have no idea.

"And *then* . . . the fur district! Where they thought I was a panhandler . . . where, I might add, you will find all kinds of strange people who still drink tea in glasses and smoke Turkish tobacco . . . where—"

He abruptly ended his runaway monologue and put Dante and the carrier down on the floor.

"My hatred for this rotten carcass," he declared, "has now grown to such proportions that I am considering suicide. Make that a murder-suicide."

And then he sat on the floor beside Dante, legs splayed. Imagine it, a grown man.

"Tony, all I can say is, I appreciate the effort."

He could only shake his head.

I filled him in on Nora's discovery of the professional relationship—at the least—between Jacobs and Mariah.

Tony stared glumly at the false cat. If he had heard what I said, he didn't make very much of it.

"Can I get you something cold to drink, Tony?"

"Drink?" He looked up at me. "Hah! I don't want drink, I want vengeance. I want wild love. I want work. I want peace. I want a villa in the Italian Alps. I want hundred-year-old brandy injected into my big toe. I want your passion forever. But a cold drink? No thank you!"

"Okay, okay. Are you staying the night?"

"No, I've got to feed the cats."

"How are Tiny and Tim?"

He made a gesture of resignation.

"What is it? Is something the matter with them?"

"No, nothing . . . nothing medical. But you know how they are. I have to be careful. If you let them get too close, they turn you into a saint or a fool for love. I wish they'd stop all that caring nonsense and just become regular house cats like your two old loonies."

The insult aside, it was a funny complaint. But I guess he had a point. Before the two Siamese went to live with Tony, they had been professionals, so to speak. They were used on occasion as companion animals, to bring cheer and relief to people in grief crisis over the loss of a loved one. They had this uncanny ability to surround you with affection—not like slavishly loyal dogs, mind you—no, it was something mysterious in their character. I don't even know how to describe it. They were just there with you, if you let them be there, close by, watching you with intense, loving concern.

Tony stood up. "I gotta go. Burn that damn thing," he ordered as he left.

Poor little Dante. I smoothed his scruffy mouton, wheeled him about for a minute, then placed him gently in his box and shut the lid.

Then I got out a yellow pad and my ballpoint pen. It was time to do a little thinking.

Aut Caesar Aut Nihil.

I wrote it down and then crossed it out. It made no sense to me. Mary Singer must have simply found that mat in a thrift shop somewhere.

Dante? Well, he made no sense, either. Just a weird toy. Some people keep their childhood teddy bears all their lives. And if Mary Singer had really brought me the toy cat to cat-sit, then she was certifiably nuts.

I wrote the names Pernell Jacobs and Flip Mariah and drew a line connecting them. Now, here was something meaty. Both actors. Worked together at least once. Each had some relationship to Mary Singer—in life or in death.

I wrote down another name: Lara Streeter. Talented actress who committed suicide during the run of *Edward the Second.* Then I joined Jacobs's and Mariah's names with hers via connecting lines.

Was there something important there? Might be.

Because Lara Streeter, like Mary Singer, suffered from weight problems.

And there was the shadowy Dr. Rodman, who dispensed amphetamines illegally. As a diet aid to Mary? Very probably.

Did the doctor also know Lara Streeter? Something to explore. Did Mariah and Jacobs have an association with Dr. Rodman?

I was criss-crossing lines in a frenzy, but getting nowhere.

While I made tea I listened to Glenn Gould playing the *Goldberg Variations*. Bach and Gould, as always, both stimulated and calmed me. Before long, I was sleeping blissfully.

I awoke at my usual time, about six-thirty in the morning. The loft was flooded with the late summer light, and already warm. Sounds beautiful, yes?

But something was wrong. No Bushy and Pancho strong-arming me about their morning feed.

In fact, neither of them was anywhere in sight.

I sat up, suddenly afraid. Had something terrible happened to them during the night?

I began a search. It didn't last long. There they were—the both of them—each sitting in his own window and staring down intently at the street.

"What's going on, guys?" I called.

They didn't move a muscle.

I padded over to the window and looked down.

Nothing there but a dog on a leash and his human companion.

"Don't worry about it," I chided the cats. "He's down there, you're up here."

It took another look to realize that the canine was a fluffy Chow and the woman holding the leash was Sam Tully's Latin-translating friend. I couldn't recall her name for a minute, but then it came back to me. Lucille Petinos.

What was she doing here? This was way out of her neighborhood—for a morning dog walk, anyway.

I moved Bushy off his ledge, opened the window, and leaned out in order to call to her: "Hello, Lucille!"

She looked up and gestured somewhat theatrically with her free hand that I should come downstairs.

I threw on clothes and went down. Once on the street, I realized I had put on bedroom slippers rather than my street shoes.

"I didn't know what to do," Lucille said in her soft voice. "I didn't know whether you'd be awake at this time."

"You didn't wake me," I assured her, pulling my foot away from the Chow, who was tugging at the tassel of my slipper. "I was still lazing in bed, but I noticed my cats staring down here. I knew they were awfully interested in something because they didn't even bug me about—"

"Sam has been shot," she said.

Tully! "Oh my God." It took me a minute to be able to speak again. "Is he . . . did they—"

"He's in St. Vincent's. He wants to see you now."

Chapter 7

They had just transferred Sam Tully from the emergency room to a regular hospital bed. He was in a room with three other patients. A nurse was taking his pulse when I walked in.

Tully yelled out when he saw me, infuriating the nurse.

I saw a few drops of blood on the elaborate white bandage on his ear.

"Are you okay, Tully? What happened?"

"Hell, yes, I'm okay. Got one of my earlobes shot off. It happened early this morning. Very early. Before the cock crowed once. Muggers. Creeps. Five or six of them. I didn't have a chance."

I drew back in horror.

"Actually, only one," he said.

Then he gave me a quick wink. He looked weary and more scruffy than ever. The nurse finished up and left.

"Got a smoke on you, Nestleton?"

"No."

"Sit on the bed—close."

I did as he had ordered. "Are you in pain?" I asked.

"A little. Listen good. Wasn't no thief. I found something, see." His voice dropped lower. "You listening, doll?"

"I'm listening, Tully. But don't exert yourself. You just came out of emergency surgery. Maybe you should just sleep now."

"Just listen! The last time I saw Mary it went like this: I heard her in the apartment, so I went down there to take her some mail I hadn't had the chance to leave in her place. When I was leaving she asked if I was headed outside. I said yeah. So she gives me some trash to take down to the street. It was almost all paper—a whole lot of paper—not newspapers or magazines, just letter paper and envelopes ripped up.

"Now, as I'm heading down the stairs I hear the phone ringing in my own apartment. So I go back up to deal with it. It was my niece's crazy husband. He got me so agitated I forgot about the bag Mary gave me. I had shoved it behind the kitchen door and forgot all about it. Until last night. It was Pickles who reminded me. Like I told you, he thinks he's a leopard. Yeah, I know you informed me that he's just a new breed of house cat, but he don't believe it. And he thinks the kitchen cabinets are part of his jungle. So he was jumping around up there and—boom—he miscalculates on one of his landings and knocks over that old bag. I shouted at him, but then remembered it was Mary's junk in there. I went over and started looking through it . . . on a chance.

"She had torn up a whole bunch of canceled checks. Lots of 'em. I start piecing some of them together. Now get this—I find *a check for six grand* made out to a meat market."

"A meat market?"

"Yeah. A plain old butcher shop. I looked 'em up in the phone book. It's over on 9th Avenue, around 38th Street."

"What could she possibly have bought at a meat market for six thousand dollars?"

"Wild, ain't it? Keep listening. Early this morning I go to the butcher shop. They're not open yet. Not to the public, anyway. But there're two guys inside getting things ready. I bang on the door and they let me in. When I ask them what they know about the check, they throw me out like the fat on a lamb chop.

"So I figure I'll go to Port Authority and get a cup of coffee, then come back later to keep an eye on them. I head up there. It's still a little dark.

"And then—boom! Somebody takes a shot at me. Lousy shot, huh? The cops in the ER said it looked like the goon was shooting to kill—aiming for the old noggin. But he missed. Got my earlobe. I told the law nothing. They think it was a crazy mugging. But listen, doll, I'm telling it to *you*—straight."

"What was the name of the place, Tully?"

"Star Market."

"Did you get the names of the men inside?"

"Nope."

"When was that canceled check dated?"

"About four months ago."

"Any other checks for that much in Mary's garbage bag?"

"Nothing even close to that one. But many of them I couldn't piece together. It was weird seeing that bag there. I mean, I forgot about it totally. Since it was just paper, it didn't stink. Real garbage would have got my notice after a couple of days."

"All right, Tully. Rest now."

"No. The locker, Nestleton."

"What locker?"

He pointed to a tall steel locker behind the bed. There was one for each patient in the room.

"Open it up. On the bottom are my shoes. Shake the left one out."

I followed his directions. The scotch-taped check fell out. I brought it back to the bed and sat down again.

"This is hot, doll."

"I think you're right," I said, confirming for myself the amount and payee. Yes, incredible as it had seemed, six thousand dollars to Star Market Butchers. What were they selling in that place, unicorn hearts?

"Now what?" Tully asked.

"Now you get some rest. I take over. We're like a tag team."

"You going to the Star Market, Nestleton?"

"Yes."

"Alone?"

"Probably."

"Be careful, doll. You gotta be careful. It was one of those characters in the store who shot me. I'm sure of it. They wanted that check back. But they didn't shoot straight. I started running before I collapsed. They had to back off. Hell, Nestleton, what's an earlobe to Harry Bondo? Did I ever tell you about the first Bondo book—*Only the Dead Do the Mambo*? In that one, Bondo took two bullets in the leg and got mauled by a Samoan wrestler and drugged by a feminist witch doctor. Didn't faze him in the least."

An aide came in with breakfast. She fastened the tray to the side of the bed. There was toast and a boiled egg, juice and jam and weak coffee. Tully wasn't eating. He had fallen fast asleep.

STAR MARKET BUTCHERS—FINE CUTS AND GAME, the sign read. I found the Star Market easily. It was exactly where Sam Tully had said it would be.

The trouble was, it was shuttered and gated—a roll-down curtain of steel covering all signs of life or commerce.

I kept looking at the sign. Game. Perhaps they did deal in unicorn hearts.

Why were they closed so early in the day? Before many other stores had even opened for business. If indeed it was someone from the market who had followed Sam and shot him, no one was the wiser. A robbery suspect was being sought, not a butcher with some perverse financial arrangement with the dead Mary Singer. But then, I realized, the shooter would not know that Sam had fabricated a story about robbery.

Next to the market was a pizza joint. Already open for business, and doing it; a few people sat at the plain tables wolfing down food. It must be a twenty-four-hour place, I reasoned. I walked in. A handsome young man was working at the counter in front of the ovens. He was twirling dough round and round, then slapping it down on the counter, punching, twirling again. His rote, disciplined movements—not to mention his beautiful forearms and wrists—were mesmerizing.

"Good morning," I said, stepping up to the counter. "Any idea why the butcher shop's closed?"

"No," he said, not missing a beat in his routine. "They were in there before. I heard 'em pulling down the gate a while ago and then they were gone."

"Do you think they'll be open again today?"

He merely shrugged.

"Can you tell me the name of the owner?"

"Who wants to know?"

"I do, sonny. I've got a big order for them."

For the first time he looked at me closely, although he went right on with his twirling and pounding. He was covered in flour dough by now. "There he is, lady."

"Where?"

"Up there on the wall . . . behind you."

There were celebrity photos all along the wall, signed by famous pizza fans who had come in over the years. There was Ed Koch and three other former New York City mayors. Sammy Davis and Bette Midler. Billy Crystal and Alan King. Even, believe it or not, Pavarotti. Catfish Hunter and Darryl Strawberry.

I was at sea. What was the young man talking about? "Who?" I finally said.

"You're asking about the owner, right? He used to be a pretty good comedian, I hear. Before he became a butcher. Or in between. Or something. Charlie Bright. Up there on your left, right next to Liza Minnelli." He laughed then. "At least that's what my uncle says. I wouldn't know. Charlie never says anything funny to me."

I moved closer to inspect the photo he had indicated. I read the inscription: "Best wishes, Charlie Bright."

I stepped back, feeling as if I'd been clubbed over the head. That's how strong the rush was.

The butcher *was* the butcher.

I recognized the lower face and neck and cast of the shoulders of the goggled chauffeur of the red Bentley—the death car. This former comedian in the glossy photo was the man who had blown Mary Singer's head off.

Detectives Warsaw and Gates sat across from me at a back booth of the pizza parlor. They had come quickly after I called.

I had ordered a slice of thin-crust pizza and a diet soda while I waited for them. But these sat untouched on the table.

"He lives on Waverly Place, in the Village," said Gates. "We sent some uniforms over, but he seems to have cleared out in a hurry. Like he shut the store in a hurry."

I handed them the ripped and mended check.

"You know what this is about," Warsaw said, handling the canceled check. It wasn't a question.

"No," I said distinctly. "That's what I came to the Star Market to find out about."

"Where'd you get it?" asked Gates.

"An anonymous donor."

"You don't say? Listen here, Miss Nestleton. You're starting to be a problem for us."

"I'm sorry. I want to be helpful."

Warsaw slid the check over to Gates, then asked me, "And you're sure that this Charlie Bright, the comic turned butcher, was the shooter that morning outside your loft?"

"That's right."

"Had you ever met him before?"

"No."

"Did you ever see him perform?"

"No."

"Ever buy meat in his store?"

"I never knew it existed until today."

"But you're certain he was the man in that chauffeur's uniform?"

"Yes."

"He was wearing big goggles, you said."

"That's right."

"And a hat."

"Yes."

"And with all that, you're still sure?"

"I've told you, yes."

"Isn't that kind of strange?"

"Why strange, Detective?"

"Well, you made a positive ID on this Bright as the shooter from an old photo even though his face, head, and body were fairly obscured on the one occasion that you saw him. But you can't give us one piece of information about the man in the backseat. Not even whether he was young or old, black or white, fat or skinny."

"Yes, you're right," I said quietly. And, for the first time, I too was wondering why that was so.

It *was* exceedingly strange that I remembered seeing only the shape of the man. Nothing else. Had I actually seen his face and repressed it? Should I volunteer to be hypnotized? Would that help?

"We'll get this sonof—this Bright," Gates said.

"I'm sure you will," I said.

"Are you going to eat that?" Warsaw asked me.

I shook my head and pushed the pizza as well as the Diet Coke across to him. He scooped up the slice, paper plate and all, but left the can on the table.

Two days later, at eleven in the morning, I was seated in one of Sam Tully's seedy bars. It was a new one to me, situated where Chinatown and Little Italy met.

There was still a bandage on his ear, but this one was much smaller than the first. "You don't like these kind of places, do you, Nestleton?" he asked, sipping a glass of beer.

"To be honest, no."

"Well, I like 'em. This is where I like to transact business, just like Pickles transacts his business on the roof."

"What business?"

"Whatever comes along."

He lit a cigarette. "Notice, Nestleton, that since you and me started hanging out together, I'm watching my health. Low-tar smokes instead of Marlboros, beer instead of bourbon."

"Yes," I said, "you're a regular health fetishist."

"Tell me something, in all honesty. You think I'm going to miss my earlobe? I mean when the dressing comes off, it'll be gone."

"I don't know, Tully. I never knew anyone who'd lost an earlobe."

"Maybe there's one of those support groups for people like me. Never been to one of those. Yep, a lost-earlobe support group. That's the ticket. Probably meets every Wednesday night—late."

"Most likely."

"What are they for, anyway, earlobes?"

"Probably nothing. They're probably vestigial," I offered.

"What about balance?"

"You mean you think earlobes balance the body?"

"Yeah, sure. Why not? Like rudders."

"They're pretty small, Tully," I noted. "Unless you're Dumbo."

"Aha. Maybe the damn things are evolutionary adaptations to wealth. Damn, how about that for a theory?"

"You're getting very philosophical."

"And you are getting morose, partner. Why? This should be a celebration. We got the shooter, didn't we?"

"Correction: we *named* the shooter—that's all. They haven't actually caught him yet. Besides, we both know the shooter is only the tip of the iceberg."

"I guess you have a point."

"Are you up to a heavy conversation, Tully?"

"Right now, I could handle sixteen tons of number nine coal—whatever that means."

I pulled out the sheet of yellow paper with the names of the parties in this mess and the crazy lines connecting them. I spread it out on the table and told Sam everything I had had no time to explain before—about *Edward the Second* and the missing pages in the *Theater Annuals* and the fact that someone had to have been watching us all quite closely—and possibly was still watching at this very moment.

"So this is the rest of the iceberg," he said.

"Yes."

"It's big and cold."

"What do you suggest?"

"Beats hell out of me."

"What would Harry Bondo do?"

Sam ordered a bourbon. He asked the bartender for one of his Marlboros. "I remember a conversation Harry had with a lady of the night. That was in book one—or was it book three?"

"A lady of the night?"

"Yeah. Bondo consorts with them."

"Shame on you, Tully."

"Harry's kind of old and ugly. What do you want?"

"That doesn't excuse it. I'm no prude, but—"

"Nestleton? Stop bugging me. I'm telling you this because what you said about icebergs reminds me of seals."

"Seals? What are you talking about, Tully?"

"Harry's conversation about seals. He always compared P.I.'s to seals."

"Is that right? Please go on with that analogy."

"Sure. Just think for a minute about seals. They swim under the ice looking for food, right? But they have to come up for air. They're not fish. So they carve out breathing holes in the ice. When they have to come up, they just look for shafts of light coming through the hole into the water. Then up they go and breathe, and everything's fine.

"*But*, seals live very dangerous lives. Because the hole they choose to pop up through to get a breath of fresh clean air might just have an Eskimo waiting with a harpoon . . . or a polar bear, for that matter. Get it?"

"Well, frankly, no. What's the point?"

"To Harry Bondo it meant you have to keep looking for those beams of light through the ice even if you get zapped when you come up for air."

"Hmm. Smart man."

"In his fashion, Nestleton."

It was strange. Ever since I had identified Charlie Bright as the gunman, I had a kind of way-out idea pulling at me, nudging, insinuating itself as a possibility. And, for some reason, Harry Bondo's seal yarn gave me confidence.

"I have an idea, Sam."

"You see? These kinds of bars get you thinking. It's a place where people philosophize. I may seem a bit down and out, honey, but you are looking at a philosopher."

"Don't congratulate me yet, Tully. This may be a long shot."

"That's the only kinda horse to bet on. Especially if you're a seal."

"Listen. We don't know who's ripping the *Edward the Second* pages out, but we do know why . . . don't we?"

"We do?"

"Yes, Tully. We do. We know there is something about the production or the cast that he or she doesn't want other people to know about. Particularly if the researcher, as I'll call that person, is connected to any investigation of Mary Singer's murder."

"Agreed, agreed. This is a breathing hole."

"So you know where I'm heading, Tully?"

"Uh-huh. This creep will go for the bait."

"Right. Eddie the Second is our bait. Maybe memorabilia, photos, diaries. Something that won't be found in public libraries."

"You're a seal and a half, doll."

"Tully, I do believe you are paying me a compliment."

"Yeah . . . well, bait is bait. What about the *trap*?"

"Maybe an ad in *Backstage* or *Variety*."

"Okay. But where is the stuff physically? Who owns the photos and diaries and stuf? Who wants to sell it? Where does the creep go in order to see it?"

"Maybe a used bookstore. Or one of those shops where they sell autographs of famous people. How about an antique store? Or even a rare record store where they still sell vinyl. Just someplace where a theater fanatic would place his collection to be sold on a commission basis. The way coin collectors use dealers to sell their treasures when the auction houses aren't interested."

"I'm following you," Sam said.

"We pay some store owner to participate in the hoax. We tell him or her what to say if anybody does take the bait and shows up: that the collection has been withdrawn from the market. Sorry. But you'll be there, Tully. With a camera. And you'll snap our visitor. And that will be that."

"What happens if more than one person shows up? What if a whole bunch of people come in asking about the stuff?"

"Photograph them all."

We contemplated our brilliance in silence for a few moment.

Finally I asked, "Now, where shall we set it up?"

"I know a junk shop."

"No, Tully, not a *junk* shop. That won't do."

"Well, Nadine calls it an antique store. But what it is is a junk shop."

"Nadine—old girlfriend?"

"Nadine's a guy. That's his last name. We used to be good buddies. Now we just get together once in a while for two-handed pinochle."

"Where's the store?"

"Fourteenth Street. Avenue A."

"What's it called?"

"The Furniture Emporium."

"Does he sell antique furniture?"

"He sells everything. If it's old and broken, he sells it. Everything from old fire hoses to wooden cream cheese crates. Girlie magazines. Empty whiskey bottles with pretty labels. Light sockets. You name it."

"Could be our man," I said. "Let's go see him."

"Don't rush me, doll. Remember, I just lost an earlobe."

*   *   *

It was one of the strangest establishments I had ever entered. A deep store, there were three architecturally distinct segments from front to back. But all differences had been dissolved by the incredible volume of . . . well, junk.

Was it fair to call Nadine's stock junk? Who knew what to call it? Take the pile of coffee tables. There were dozens of them, some hanging on the walls. They were all in disrepair—marred, splintered, burned, wounded in some fundamental way.

As for the proprietor, Sam's friend Nadine, he was every bit as strange as the store. Short, stocky, at least as old as Tully, he was bald and had a formidable handlebar mustache. He was wearing a rumpled cowboy shirt. He looked a bit ferocious, but he was actually almost dysfunctionally shy, rarely saying a word, and when he did talk it was in a mumble. That assertive mustache did not suit him at all.

When Sam introduced us Nadine nodded and said something—maybe—but I never figured out what it was.

"We need some help," Tully explained.

Nadine shrugged.

A woman emerged from behind a disabled bookcase. She was pulling a dusty carton behind her. "Why don't you put prices on anything?" she demanded angrily. She reached into the carton and pulled out several issues of what appeared to be an old German-language periodical of the scholarly rather than the popular variety.

"You've got thirty of these," she said in a scolding tone. "How much for each one?"

Nadine, refusing to look directly at the customer, managed to croak out: "A dollar twenty-five."

"*Apiece?*" the woman asked.

He nodded.

The two of them stepped over to the counter to consummate the transaction.

"You'll get used to him," Tully told me.

The woman left the store with the entire contents of the carton. Tully and I had heard her say she'd take ten of the journals, but Nadine must have made her an offer she couldn't refuse if she bought the lot. He may have been painfully shy, but he obviously was able to rouse himself once in a while into sharp salesmanship.

We joined Nadine at the counter. He was sitting on a metal stool, looking all in, as if the transaction had taken his last ounce of strength. It was very warm in the store. I noticed some antique muskets and a battered fireplace screen hanging on the wall behind him. Higher up on the same wall were several World War II-era pinup calendars.

Nadine turned his weary eyes to Tully.

"We've got a sting operation going, old buddy. A beauty. But we need you to pull it off."

Nadine moved his glance from Tully to the cash register to the rusted Mr. Peanut can on the counter and then to me. His head moved from side to side like an old walrus grazing for moss on a rock. Was he the real reason Harry Bondo spoke in seal meta-phors? But a seal is not a walrus.

He repeated the phrase Tully had used, "a sting operation," making it sound like a foreign language.

"You tell him, doll," Tully said.

I outlined the plan, emphasizing the fact that he, Nadine, would be required to do nothing except to tell any person inquiring about the fictitious collection that it had been summarily withdrawn from the market, and that he could answer no further questions.

Sam interrupted me once, leaning across the counter and fairly shouting at Nadine: "You got it? We're flushing out a killer, man."

Then he turned to me. "By the way, who do you think we'll catch?"

"Pernell Jacobs, I suppose. Or Flip Mariah. Or per-haps the comic butcher who shot you. Maybe it will be Cora Rodman. Or maybe even Lara Streeter."

"I thought she was dead. You told me she killed herself in '85."

"Lots of ghosts around, Tully," I replied. "You never know."

Nadine leaned across the counter and studied Sam's bandaged ear, noticing it, apparently, for the first time. He took it in without comment.

"Yeah, the bastards shot my lobe off," Sam said poisonously.

No answer from Nadine.

"Nadine's our man," Tully said confidently. "You

can trust him, Nestleton. And when this is all over we'll go to his place on Waverly and get some eggs. Nobody makes scrambled eggs like Nadine—nobody."

"That's funny," I noted. "The detectives told me that Charlie Bright lives on Waverly Place, too."

"Where on Waverly?"

"They didn't say."

"Nadine here has the distinction of living at Waverly and Waverly," Sam said proudly.

"Don't be ridiculous," I said. "There is no such intersection."

He turned to his silent buddy. "Will you listen to her! She's telling me where you live. Do you live at the corner of Waverly and Waverly or not?"

We received a firm nod.

"But listen, Tully. That would mean there are two different Waverly Places downtown that go their separate ways but meet up at least once."

"Yeah, that's right."

"But I've lived in New York City for a long time now, a lot of that time in or near the Village. And I've never heard of any *two* Waverly Places."

"Life is full of surprises, doll."

We bid good-bye to Nadine. I offered my hand for him to shake, but got only another nod in return.

"Oh, just a minute, Tully!" I said when we were outside again. "We forgot to discuss payment with him."

"He didn't say anything. Let it alone."

"But he doesn't seem to say anything, period. Maybe he was waiting for us to bring it up."

"When Nadine wants money he'll ask for it. Believe me."

Then Tully took a great gulp of the humid air. "Do you feel it, doll?" he asked.

"Feel what?"

"The thrill. The chase. The game. The *heat*! Oh, honey, we're deep in it now!"

"Sure, Tully. But first I need to buy a new Bic pen. Do you have any change?"

We were in a bar that Sam Tully had selected as the ideal venue to compose a bogus ad. The place was so seedy I felt that unseen forces were about to steal my shoes.

It was located on Christopher Street just east of the now-defunct Lion's Head, which had for years been known as a "writers' bar." Not Sam's kind of place, of course. No, this dim and faintly menacing pub a few doors away was more his style.

"I got a pad," Sam announced, "and a fancy Mont-Blanc Rolling Writer pen my niece sent me one Christmas. Never even used it before. We're in business."

"I'm impressed. But Tully, maybe I should write the ad."

"You're crazy. *I'm* the writer, Nestleton."

"As you wish."

"The way I figure it, we do it methodically. We got only one shot—right?"

"Right."

"Maybe some jukebox music. You want to hear something?"

"I don't care."

He went to the jukebox and put on Billie Holiday.

"I figure we need something intense in the background, to get us revved up," he said, whipping out his pen and opening a little notebook.

"Yes. Intense," I agreed.

"Point by point, Nestleton."

"Right, Sam."

"Where is the ad appearing?"

"*Backstage, Variety, Footlights*. You know, trade papers that mostly people in the theater would pick up."

"How many words?"

"Fifty or less."

"First the headline."

"Right."

"Give me an idea, Nestleton."

"Okay. How about FOR SALE: RARE THEATRICAL MEMORABILIA?"

"Not bad."

He wrote it down. He studied it. "I like it," he announced. "Now what?"

"Well," I said, "let's make it simple. Something like—'Fifty years of Broadway history. Cast photos, programs, diaries, directors' scripts from *A View from the Bridge, Foxhole in the Parlor, A Raisin in the Sun, Edward the Second, Hurly Burly*, and dozens more. View them at the Furniture Emporium, 14th St. & Ave. A, on Wednesday, 10-12 A.M. Must sell. No serious offer refused.' "

"I got it! I got it! All of it, Nestleton. Let me have a drink and I'll do some polishing. You did good, but a little pizzazz would help. You know, for a lady who babysits cats, you have a way with words."

"Thank you, Tully. But my primary profession is acting."

He had his drink. He started working furiously with his roller-ball pen.

"Okay. Here's the final copy," he said when he had finished his labors. "The revised copy, as we say in the publishing game."

He read it back to me. It was virtually word for word what I had composed.

"Excellent editing, Tully. You added just the right touch."

"What next, doll?"

"I place the ads and pay for them. You buy the Polaroid and pay for that."

"Check."

"In seventy-two hours, Sam, someone is going to walk into the Furniture Emporium to view the collection."

"Got ya. I'll be waiting. In the shadows. *Click, click.* Old Sam Tully, war correspondent. Nestleton, this has the feel of success. That creep is about to crawl out from under his rock. It's gonna work! We're a helluva team."

For some reason his optimism depressed me. Yes, it was our best—and only—shot. It made sense, but . . .

"Want to party, doll?"

"I *beg* your pardon." I must have sounded like Franklin Pangborn, eyes bucked, brows reaching for the sky.

Sam Tully laughed and laughed.

Chapter 8

The trap was set. The juicy bogus bait was flaunted in the classified pages of all the theatrical tabloids. The camera was readied. The proprietor of the Furniture Emporium was briefed once again. Yes, all was ready.

And what a glorious late-summer morning it turned out to be. Dark and cool, distant rumbles of thunder.

The city seemed to balance precariously between the two rivers. One really felt that Manhattan was an island—perhaps even a volcanic island that could be thrust higher or sent tumbling beneath the waters.

Sam Tully and I arrived at the Furniture Emporium at eight o'clock in the morning.

Nadine was drinking a container of black coffee that smelled as if it had licorice in it, and consuming one of the largest cheese danishes ever baked or assembled.

Only one task remained, and that was to find a secure, out-of-the-way niche from which Sam could use the Polaroid without being seen.

Actually this task turned out to be quite easily accomplished, given the profusion of junk in Nadine's establishment. We simply moved together two hulking armoires—rooming-house-style items that must have dated back to the 1920s—and that was that. One of them had virtually no back anymore; it had rotted away to form a natural latticework, and with the front half-open Sam could shoot through the space easily without being seen. The niche was only ten feet or so from the counter where Nadine would inform the would-be customer that the collection had suddenly and without explanation been withdrawn from the market by its anonymous owner.

At nine-thirty I left the store. Nadine and I wished each other luck.

The plan was for Sam to meet me at the post office on 14th Street, a block from the Emporium, between twelve noon and twelve-thirty. That meant I had almost three hours to kill.

So I strolled down Avenue A, usually pulsating with life, but uncommonly calm that morning. I was calm, too, extremely calm, even though I had the bizarre feeling that someone was following me. I turned once or twice, looked over my shoulder as I made my way past the bodegas and the bars and the burned-out tenements and the new housing in mid-construction. No one was there.

At 9th Street I turned west and walked into the Cafe Gigi, a place I'd gone a few times before.

There were very few customers inside. I sat down

at a table near the door. The waitress approached with a menu, but I waved it off and started to order a cappuccino.

Suddenly I switched gears and blurted out, "Pancakes and sausages—and a cappuccino."

I realized I hadn't had a good meal for days. Only snacks and tidbits and salads—rabbit food, as Nora called it. Now was the time to stoke the engine. And Gigi's made spectacular thin buttermilk pancakes, mottled to perfection. Their sausages were pretty good, too.

The waitress brought the cappuccino first. Five minutes later the food arrived.

Oh my! The platter was lovely! Three delicate flapjacks and an equal number of fat little sausages. I laid on the butter and syrup with absolute abandon, then dug in.

The meal was delicious. I ate it quickly and with gusto. A cooling breeze coming in through the open door fueled my appetite, and for a moment I contemplated ordering something more.

But then that sensation of being watched returned. I looked up suddenly.

The pretty young waitress was standing quite close to me, openly staring at me. Was I eating like a condemned man? Had I dribbled syrup down my blouse? Was my face smeared? Embarrassed, I reached for a napkin.

"I know you," the girl announced quietly.

I studied her carefully. She was in her late twenties, I estimated—short, trim, vivacious-looking, with long black hair pulled up in a deliberately untidy bun. She did not look familiar at all. But then I remembered about the infamous video taken by Flip Mariah. I steeled myself for another round of curiosity and pity.

"You don't remember me, I guess," the girl stated.

"No."

"Aren't you Alice Nestleton?"

"That's right."

"I thought so. I thought it was you. But you've changed. I was in the class you taught at the New School."

So that was it. But I didn't remember the face. After all, it was almost five years ago. As for my having changed—well, I had put on a few pounds and was wearing my hair shorter, a few silver strands visible.

"Do you remember the name of the course?" she asked.

What a peculiar question. Of course I did. I had called it "The New York Actor." It was a mélange, but mostly it was about how to survive in the theatrical jungle. I had intended it as a practical guide for young people who wanted to act: What to look for in an acting coach. How to look for work. How to audition. In short, the nuts and bolts of the profession.

"Thank you for remembering me," I said.

To my surprise, her face clouded over. What had I said wrong?

She moved even closer. "You didn't tell the truth."

"What are you talking about?"

"You didn't tell us how sad the whole thing is."

"Look. It's a tough business. I made that clear, didn't I? Tough, yes . . . but sad?"

Her accusation angered me, even though I didn't know what she meant by "sad." But then I just felt stupid. Here I was, embarked on a crucial operation pertaining to the Mary Singer tragedy, and a waitress who was really an out-of-work actress was taking me to task for something I had said or failed to say to a class of hopefuls five years ago.

She looked around for the boss, saw that he was busy, and felt safe in sitting down across from me.

She leaned over: "I just want to say something to you. I know you're a fine actress. And I really liked your class. But, look, I'm not interested in making movies. I really don't give a damn about being rich and famous. I don't want to do soap operas. I don't want to make commercials. What I want is a company of players. And I can't find them. Do you know what I'm saying? That's what I mean when I say it's sad. I want to play many roles—all kinds of roles. I want to learn. I want to be part of a rollicking, crazy, fullblown theater company. I want to live with people who love the theater . . . who play for audiences that need theater. That's all. A company of players."

She stood up suddenly. "Why am I carrying on like this? Oh, God. . . . I'm sorry."

She ripped the check out of her pad and placed it face down on my table. Then she walked away.

I was stunned. There were tears in my eyes. Sad? Yes. I did know what she was talking about. I knew what she was going through.

The sticky remains of my repast now seemed loathsome. I paid the bill and rushed outside.

What a ridiculous confrontation! What a bizarre interlude. Once again my past had popped up. There had never been a more idealistic young actress than Alice Nestleton, fresh from Minnesota, wandering the mean streets of the Big City. There had never been a young actress more determined to find a company of players, as that girl had put it.

I killed the next two hours just walking around slowly, trying to regain my focus, trying not to think of all those gifted young actors who would never find that company of players, because, as someone once put it, "there ain't no such animal anymore."

At five minutes before noon I walked into the post office on 14th Street and stationed myself at one of the high writing tables.

After I'd been standing there about ten minutes, a uniformed postal police officer began to regard me with suspicion. I grabbed a slip from the desk, picked up one of the pens attached to the desk by a chain, and began to fill out a change-of-address form. The officer quickly lost interest.

Sam Tully walked into the post office at twelve-forty. He swaggered in—to be more accurate, a young man's swagger at that—with a smile on his face. The old geezer had struck pay dirt! I could tell.

He walked up to the table, right beside me, reached into his back pocket, pulled out three snapshots, and simply dropped them on the desk.

"Don't you love it, Nestleton?" he whispered. Then he spread them out for easy viewing.

He tapped the first one. I looked down at it. It was of a portly gentleman, quite old.

"He was interested in any stuff about Montgomery Clift," Sam said. "It seems that play you mention in the ad—*Foxhole in the Parlor*—was Clift's first Broadway show. Anyway, when Nadine told him nothing was for sale any longer, he just turned and walked out. Do you know him?"

I looked closely at the photograph. It definitely wasn't Pernell Jacobs or Charlie Bright. The man pictured was too old to be Flip Mariah. And he wasn't anyone I knew in or out of the theater. Though he did bear a vague resemblance to my niece's boyfriend Felix.

"And this lady," Sam said, pointing to the second picture, "didn't say much. She just wanted to look at everything available. Tough broad. After your pal Nadine told her the collection had been yanked from circulation, she called Nadine an idiot for bringing her down there on a wild-goose chase. Recognize her?"

I looked down briefly at the photo, then did a double-take. Did you ever feel the blood literally drain from your face?

Yes. I recognized her, all right. But I guess I didn't really *know* her at all. Not if I could believe my eyes. I didn't answer Sam's question. I just couldn't deal with it yet.

"And what about the last one?" I asked, dazed. The young man in the snapshot was dressed in a white linen suit.

"He's a French tourist," said Tully. "Said he was just looking. Couldn't understand him too well."

I turned away from the photos and stared at the people waiting on line for a postal teller.

"What's the matter, honey?" asked Sam. "You sick?"

"No!"

I turned back. He tapped the third photograph, the one of the Frenchman.

"No," I replied. "But I do know . . . her." I picked up snapshot number two.

"All right!" Sam said triumphantly. "So who is it?"

"Her name is Nora Karroll. My friend Nora."

At two-thirty that afternoon I was standing with Sam Tully in tow outside the Pal Joey Bistro in the theater district. The lunch crowd was emptying out.

I just stood there, staring inside. I knew why I was standing there. But I didn't know what to do next.

A holy mess! as my grandmother used to say. This

thing with Nora was a mess. But it was worse. It was an inexplicable mess . . . a festering, confusing, and dangerous turn of events.

Sam asked, "We going to stand here on the sidewalk all afternoon, Nestleton? If so, maybe I can rent us a couple of beach chairs."

"Let's go in," I said suddenly.

Sam followed me into the restaurant. Nora was nowhere to be seen. That was strange, since she did everything in her place from seating customers to refilling the bar shelves with whiskey and overseeing the kitchen.

The bartender waved to me and pointed toward her office. I nodded my thanks.

The door to the office was closed, which was even stranger, because it was a steam box in there in summer unless the door was open to receive the cooled air from the system in the main dining room.

I knocked, and we walked in. Nora was on her posh chair behind the desk, trying to nap.

"Leave the door open!" she ordered, seeming to emerge from a fitful dream. "Oh, it's you, Alice. How are you?"

"Nora, this is my friend Sam Tully."

"Then welcome," she said, smiling. "How about a drink?"

"No," I answered.

"I wasn't talking to you, dear." She looked over questioningly at Sam, but he also declined.

"Sam has been helping me," I told her.

"Yeah? With what?"

"The Mary Singer thing."

She laughed. "I thought Tony and I were your assistants with that. You sure have a lot of help on this one, don't you? Now all you need is a cat-sitter for *your* cats. They must be feeling a little neglected these days."

She turned to Sam Tully. "Do you do that, too?"

He bristled and said, "I only cat-sit for leopards."

"Look, Nora," I said, "you and Tony didn't seem too enthusiastic about getting involved with this case."

"Oh, is that so? Didn't I go to the library for you to get that information? Didn't I do my part?"

I hesitated before responding. Nora was playing dumb. She was acting way out of character.

"Were you downtown this morning, Nora?" I asked directly.

"No."

I took in the lie without comment, realizing there was no way to finesse this. I nodded to Sam.

He extracted the Polaroid shot of her and placed it wordlessly on the desk in front of her. Of course I did not know what effect it was having on Nora, but to me the photo seemed to pulsate with threat.

She stared at the image of herself for the longest time before reaching for it. When finally she did pick it up, she ripped it slowly to pieces.

"Nora," I said deliberately, when she was finished, "please tell me what is going on."

She was silent.

"Nora," I repeated, "you have to talk to me. You *must*."

Her blank stare seemed to ask me why.

"I'm your friend," I said in answer to the unspoken question.

Again, she refused to speak. I wanted to grab her and shake the voice out of her.

"Did you have anything to do with Mary Singer's death, Nora? Are you involved in it?"

At last she replied. "No," she said, almost inaudibly. Then she began to shout it in a kind of drone: "No, no, no!" She stood up.

Sam Tully slammed the door shut. I moved quickly to Nora's side, behind the desk. She was trembling something awful.

"Sit down," I said, guiding her back down on the chair. She had begun to weep now and was trying hard to stifle her cries.

"Why, Nora?" I asked gently. "Why did you go to that shop today? What were you doing? Did you rip the pages out of that book?"

She was nodding—yes to all my questions.

"But why?"

"I had a walk-on in *Edward the Second*."

I waited for her to go on, to explain, and when she did not I asked in genuine puzzlement: "So what? What does that have to do with anything? Why would you tear those pages out and why did you go to the Furniture Emporium?"

"I—I didn't want you to know."

"Know what, dear?"

"That I knew Flip Mariah. That he and I were lovers."

"Oh," I said. "But, still, so what?"

"Alice! Don't you understand?"

"No. No, I don't. But I want to understand. Explain it, Nora . . . please."

"Send him out," she ordered suddenly, pointing to Sam.

I shook my head. "I can't do that, Nora. Be sensible. What is going on?"

She held her hands up, palms out, signaling that she would tell me . . . that she would speak the truth . . . that she only needed a moment to compose herself.

Tully and I waited. Nora kept folding and unfolding her hands. Then she swept the tatters of the photo into the wastebasket.

"Alice, do you know where it was that I learned to cook?"

"Of course I do. You told me when we ran into each other again after all those years. You went to France, to one of those grand schools for chefs."

"I lied."

"You did?"

"Yes."

"All right. So where did you learn?"

"I learned how to cook in a women's prison in upstate New York. Where I was serving a three-year sentence. I am a convict, Alice. Do you understand what I'm saying?"

"I don't believe you. You're making it up."

"I'm not. It's the truth."

"Why were you in prison?"

"Because of Flip Mariah. He got me a job in a Broadway theater selling tickets. There was a smash musical. A giant hit. I sold the tickets to a shill at box office prices. Then he and Flip scalped the tickets at enormous profits.

"Flip cheated the shill out of a bundle. The guy wanted to get back at him, so he went to the DA. I was arrested. I didn't implicate Flip. And he didn't help me. The sentence was severe because I wouldn't talk. And because I didn't know that while scalping tickets is only a misdemeanor, an employee of a Broadway theater who knowingly diverts tickets into the hands of a scalper is guilty of a felony. In my case I diverted at least two hundred and fifty thousand dollars' worth of tickets at box office prices. As for that mastermind, Flip Mariah, he never once came to see me in prison. I never saw or spoke to him again."

She stood up then. "Oh my God, Alice! I just couldn't tell you. I didn't want you to learn I had that bit part in *Edward*. I didn't want you to know I was a felon. I didn't want you to know about Flip and me. Can't you understand?"

"It's okay, Nora. Everything's okay now." I put my arms around her. "Sam, get her some water."

I tried to remember the almost miraculous reunion I had had with Nora a few years back, which had happened by chance. It had been so long since we'd seen each other. I'd told her what I'd been doing in the years since we'd last met, and she had reciprocated. Never for a moment had I doubted the truth of her autobiographical descriptions. It never occurred to me to question them. What a naif I had been.

Sam brought the water, but Nora didn't drink it.

"That's why I went to that store on Fourteenth Street, Alice. I saw that ad. It said they were selling memorabilia about the 1985 performance of *Edward the Second*. I had to see if I was in any of the cast photos. I'd have done anything to keep you from knowing. I thought maybe you'd seen the ad, too. I thought I could close that door for good. I didn't want you to know about prison, Alice. More than anything else, I didn't want you to know I had lied to you.

"When you sent me to the library to find information on Flip and Pernell Jacobs, I thought it would be best to tell the truth. I knew they were in *Edward the Second* together. I thought you would stop there. So I just ripped out those pages. But you didn't stop—you wouldn't. I was stupid; I should have known you wouldn't."

"I placed that ad, Nora."

She nodded. "I see. This is all so sordid . . . so awful."

"Did you lie to me about Mary Singer?" It was such a hard thing to make myself say, but I had to ask. I had to know.

"No! I swear, I told you the truth. I didn't have anything to do with that woman's death."

"Do you know where Flip Mariah is now?"

"No."

"Do you have any idea where Pernell Jacobs is now?"

"None."

"And you're sure you have had no contact at all with Mariah since you went to prison?"

"Yes."

"She's lying," Sam said quietly. His words struck home.

Nora flung her hands up. "Okay! Okay! There was one other time. But we didn't meet—or even talk. He sent me twenty thousand dollars for keeping my mouth shut. That's how I opened Pal Joey.

"But, Alice, listen. I had no idea he was going to give me that money. I kept quiet out of love. Understand? Out of love. I loved that miserable bastard more than I ever loved any man before or since."

That was all she would or could say. She sank down on the chair again, spent.

There was nothing more we could do there. Sam and I walked out of the bistro and into the afternoon heat.

"We went up for air at the wrong damn breathing hole," Harry Bondo's creator noted.

We headed toward 8th Avenue, slowly.

"I don't know what to do next," I murmured.

"Well, Nestleton, I gotta see a man about a horse. Keep in touch." And with that, Tully turned up the avenue.

I walked downtown in the heat. At 34th Street I turned left, toward 7th Avenue, figuring to get a bus home.

Macy's! It loomed up in front of me. Air conditioning! Yes, I needed some relief. The moment I walked through the revolving doors and into the store, I was jolted by the blast of cold air. It was glorious. I wandered aimlessly among the men's clothing.

A sign announcing a tie sale caught my eye. Rack upon rack of them, all over the countertops. All kinds of ties, specially priced at forty-nine dollars apiece. A bit steep, I thought. It must be expensive to dress a man today.

Then the idea of buying a nice tie for Basillio came to me. I wondered how many ties poor Nora had purchased for Flip Mariah during their time together.

One tie in particular caught my fancy. It was dark red silk with tiny soft yellow birds flying about in formation.

I indulged myself caressing the fabric for a few minutes, then headed for another rack down at the other end of the counter.

I had to stop short. A man had beaten me to the rack. He was about five feet away from me, running his hand across the surface of one of the ties.

But his eyes were not on the silken fabric. No. His eyes were on me.

And there was the slightest hint of a smile at the corners of his lips.

I took a step backward, startled.

I was looking at a tall, well-muscled, middle-aged black man. Very well dressed, almost dandyish, with graying hair at the sides of his large sculpted head.

My cardiovascular system began to execute an elaborate series of flips.

Pernell Jacobs?

No. Yes. No.

I looked around wildly. But he never moved. Should I call the police? What would I say?

Should I scream? Why?

I turned away from him. But then I turned back, deciding that I had to face him.

"Is that you, Pernell?" I finally spoke the simple words. Not loudly, not whispered. As if we were again rehearsing a scene we'd done together more than twenty years ago.

He did not answer me.

I suddenly remembered waiting in the downtown cafe with the unhappy actress. I recalled how I had the sense of being followed. Had that been Pernell shadowing me?

"Are you Pernell Jacobs?" I said deliberately, my voice much sharper than before.

Still he didn't answer. It had been so long since I'd seen him up close . . . I just couldn't be sure.

Time disfigures memory. Bodies change, not to mention faces.

I found it harder and harder to breathe. The air conditioning, so welcome a few minutes ago, was now strangling me.

In desperation, I suddenly shouted out: "Mary Singer!" Now, *that* was loud. Too loud. People were beginning to stare. I cringed. Meanwhile, Pernell—or whoever he was—was calmly walking away.

A security man in a blue blazer carrying the ubiquitous walkie-talkie seemed to materialize out of nowhere. "Is there a problem, Miss?"

"No, no problem," I said, brushing past him and heading out of the store. On my way, I passed the rack of ties that the would-be Pernell had been exploring. I saw the one he had been so interested in. He had made a tight knot in it.

Oh God. A hangman's knot.

I rushed outside and headed downtown at breakneck speed. He had warned me. He had threatened me.

But was it really Pernell Jacobs? And was the knot in that tie really a noose?

I slowed, aching all over. I was drenched in perspiration. And I realized that I really didn't know who and what I had seen in Macy's.

Take it easy, Alice, I cautioned myself. It was most likely a case of mad dogs and Englishmen in the midday sun.

Focus on what is real . . . on what can be grasped with two hands.

An hour later—stunned and disgusted—I was back in the loft with Bushy and Pancho.

I sat at my dining table eating Afrika cookies: tiny imported chocolate-covered wafers that for some reason were always on special sale at my neighborhood supermarket. With them I drank 2 percent milk.

When I need to clear my head, I often resort to fancy cookies.

When both head and heart are in trouble, I add cold milk to the therapy.

The kitties stared up hungrily at me. Oh, they loved milk, even the 2 percent variety. But like so many others, I heeded the vets' injunction against giving them milk.

It's strange how times change. My grandmother's and my many felines were literally raised on milk. Not the low-fat variety; fresh, warm, nonhomogenized, nonpasteurized whole milk direct from a cow's udder, splashed into a dented old bucket.

I finished all the cookies. Ashamed of my greed, I poured a little of the milk on the floor in front of each of the cats. They lapped it up happily—and wanted more.

"No, sorry," I told them. "That's it."

Should I call Nora? Should I try to console her?

I read the print on the milk container, then placed it back on the table and began to savage the empty cookie package. Just like Nora ripping up the photograph of herself, I thought.

I wasn't really angry at her. I was hurt. Not because she had lied to me about her past. Everybody does. I have never, ever told the truth to anyone about the misery of my brief foray into the marital state.

No, it wasn't Nora's lie that distressed me. It was the fact that she thought I would terminate our friendship if I knew she had been a jailbird, a thief, and a fool in the past.

That demeaned me. I believe in the Ten Commandments, but everyone slips up once in a while.

How could I have appeared to be such a straitlaced holy roller to her? It was hard to fathom.

Oh, what a miserable day it had been! The brilliantly planned, meticulously laid, daringly executed trap had only caught poor Nora.

The only thing that came out of the debacle was the confirmation that Flip Mariah was indeed an actor gone bad.

As for that Pernell Jacobs sighting—or mirage—in Macy's, either it was real and he had been following me and the knot in the tie was indeed a death threat. Or he was just a tall handsome stranger who had seen me on TV or onstage and was smiling at the memory.

Either way, there was nothing I could do now.

Bushy moaned. He wanted more milk. He pleaded

for more. Even crazy Pancho was giving me one of those "have pity" looks.

"No," I said firmly, "but I promise you that one day I will put you both in a car and drive upstate to a dairy farm where I'll buy you a pail of fresh warm milk."

They didn't believe me. How sad it is, I thought, that Bushy and Pancho have never tasted that rich sweet nectar.

Sad? That bloody word again! That waitress! I realized she had annoyed me more than Nora. She had literally accused me of lying about the New York theater world in a course about the same.

I calmed down. That girl was in a fantasy world . . . her and her "company of players" . . . seeking to live theater rather than slip in and out of a role. The fantasy of a very young person.

Ah . . . the tears just rolled down my face. Of course we all had that fantasy. But in the early seventies many wonderful experimental repertory companies still existed. There was a possibility.

I laid my head down on the table and closed my eyes. A flood of memories came back to me: when I was a young actress in New York, just like her; those years at the Dramatic Workshop, where I first met Tony and Nora and Joseph Grablewski and Pernell Jacobs and—well, who could remember them all.

Yes, they were the best of times. Everything was exciting, subversive, infused with importance. The great Method actors and directors of the 1950s had laid the groundwork. The rock explosion of the 1960s had swept away most of the stupid censorship laws. We all felt a new kind of theater was about to emerge—it seemed imminent. We were true believers.

Alas, it never came to pass. But what different times they were. Actors like Brando and Kim Stanley and a host of others were not prancing celebrities; they were sources of wisdom, light, courage. They taught us how to listen . . . how to kiss . . . how to drink whiskey straight . . . how to walk across the stage in a slip.

I remembered the nights in those bars along 8th Avenue, talking wildly about the most minute and esoteric things in a performance—every beautiful nuance.

I remembered my first term at the Dramatic Workshop. Oh! The teachers had it in for me. I was too tall, too blonde, too pretty, too farm-girlish. That I had a great deal of acting experience was totally discounted.

And Grablewski used to torment me the most, which is probably why I fell for him so hard and so futilely. He was a mesmerizing, witty, go-for-the-jugular teacher before the drink got to him.

I recalled one class in particular. Grablewski was in rare form. He started out with his usual attack on mendacity, fakery, and God knows what else in the American theater.

Then he attacked specific actors.

Then he got down to business.

"Suppose," he said, "Sidney Kingsley gives you a new script. No, not *Detective Story*. This one is *The Whore's Story*. Suppose he gives it to *you*, Miss Nestleton."

"Why would he give it to her?" someone piped up.

"Who knows?" Grablewski answered. "Playwrights are crazy. Anyway, the main character in the play, Miss Nestleton, is a very loose woman. In fact, a high-priced prostitute. How, Miss Nestleton, are you going to deal with the situation? I presume you're a virgin."

He waited for an answer.

"I think that's my business," I finally said, my face flaming red.

"Wrong, Miss Nestleton. It's the audience's business. And your fellow actors' business. But, anyway, enlighten us, *Miss* Nestleton, as to how you will prepare your whore's role."

"Like I would prepare any other role," I replied.

"Wrong again, Miss Nestleton. There is no way you can legitimately create this role."

He paused and let his eyes roam the class. Everyone waited for the punch line.

"Pardon me. There *is* one way. And that way is the route great artists take. You deal first and foremost with the contradiction."

All our faces went blank. What the hell was he talking about?

"First," he continued, "you identify the contradiction, which is . . . simply . . . how can a corn-fed, naive young Minnesota virgin play a hip urban pay-for-play chick? That is the contradiction. And that is the focus of your preparation. You fasten on it like a bulldog. You use it to pull out of your past feelings and memories that you never knew were there. You craft the role around that contradiction. You . . ."

I lifted my head from the table. My eyes were still wet. Those old memories were both painful and exhilarating. Particularly the acting classes with Grablewski. Him and *his* contradiction—the man knew more facts about theater than anyone on earth, but he loved to play with elusive concepts. Yes. Grablewski and his contradiction.

I sat up very straight. Suddenly something was bothering me, to put it mildly.

When I had finally located Grablewski in the coffeehouse called Bookers and found him sober, he had told me all he knew about Pernell Jacobs and Flip Mariah. He had been specific, as he always was. He had named productions that only a handful of people attended, and the year in which each one took place.

But he had not mentioned *Edward the Second*.

Not a single mention of that production. How was that possible? It was a famous, or more accurately infamous, mounting of the play, on account of Lara Streeter's suicide. Sure—the years of alcoholism had eaten into Grablewski's memory. But he remembered everything else, didn't he? Why not *Edward the Second*?

I looked at the clock. It was five-forty. I called Sam Tully, who picked up on the first ring.

"You sound tired, Tully."

"I am tired. Who is this?"

"Nestleton," I said officiously.

"Your voice is weird."

"I got something, Tully."

"Whaddya mean?"

"Something important. Something I just put together."

"You don't say."

"Yes, I do. We have to go back uptown."

"To your pal's bistro?"

"No. To a place called Bookers. A coffee shop not far from Nora's bistro."

"When?"

"In an hour. I'll be downstairs in an hour. We'll take a cab up there."

"You sure you got something this time?"

"Oh, I'm sure all right."

The taxi ride up was slow. Sam found it hard to concentrate as I told him about the new development.

"You don't give up, do you, honey?" he commented when I had finished recounting the story.

"Not this time."

"It's like Harry Bondo once said: 'For some babes, the party never ends.' "

"This is no party, Tully."

He laughed ruefully. "No, I guess it ain't." Then he lit a cigarette.

The driver instructed him in no uncertain terms to put it out—"It's the law," he added self-righteously.

Sam cursed under his breath, rolled his eyes, and touched his bandaged ear as if showing it off to the cabbie, but then flung the butt out of the window.

"How do you know this old alkie Rakowski, or whatever the hell his name is, is going to be there right now?"

"He's not a drunk anymore, and his name is Grablewski—as if you didn't remember. And I know he's there because . . . well, because it's where he hangs out these days."

"You're sure he's in on it, huh?"

"Yes. Didn't you hear what I just told you? I gave you the whole story. He deliberately withheld information from me that he had to possess."

"What does that prove?"

"Concealment is the mother of homicide," I said, rather surprised that the ridiculous homily had popped into my mind.

"Harry Bondo can use that one, Nestleton. I'm gonna put it in my next book. If there ever is another one."

When we reached Bookers I led Sam inside and onto the takeout line in the front alcove.

From there we could see the dining area but not be seen.

"Who *are* all these people?" he asked.

"Bit players . . . comics . . . strippers. The would-be's. Those who couldn't make it in the greasepaint but couldn't get out."

"I kinda like the looks of 'em," he said.

"Then look over there," I said. "By the wall."

"The guy in the old suit writing in a notebook?"

"That's him. That's Joseph Grablewski."

"What's he so caught up with?"

"He's writing a play."

I took Tully's arm and pulled him outside.

"What are you doing, Nestleton? I thought you wanted to talk to this guy."

"Suddenly, Tully, I just don't know what to do. And I'm frightened. What if he just says he forgot about that production? What if he says—"

"Hold it!"

I stopped my out-of-control monologue. "What?"

"You're getting worked up again, doll. Let's calm down here. He's inside. We're outside."

"Sam, I *know* he's involved. Deep in it. I just know it."

"Are you sure it ain't some kind of payback on your part, honey? Like you said, he used to both turn on you and turn you on. That's a wicked, wicked formula, Nestleton. Sure you're not just getting even?"

"I'm sure."

"Then we need a plan."

"A plan, yes. I can't afford another debacle like the Furniture Emporium sting."

"You know what Harry Bondo would do?"

"No. What?"

"He'd wait until this Grablewski fella goes home. Find out where he's living. Then, next morning, Bondo waits until the guy goes out again and lets himself into the pad and takes a good long look around."

"You mean a break-in."

"I guess you could call it that."

"No. That's going too far. That puts us on the wrong side of the fence, Tully. We're supposed to be the good guys, remember."

"What fence are you talking about? I don't see no fence. Like Bondo says in . . . I forget which book . . . 'You can always clean a rusty pipe with a rusty Brillo pad.' "

I didn't get the wisdom of the quote, but I did see the wisdom of the plan. In the end, I agreed to the break-in.

We waited three hours and twenty-one minutes, most of that time spent in a nearby shoe store, for Grablewski to leave the safety of Bookers. When he emerged he went directly home—which turned out to be a dingy four-story brownstone in Hell's Kitchen, only two blocks from the Star Market. Both Tully and I noted the coincidence.

Then Sam and I had two stiff drinks apiece and went to our respective homes to sleep. The cat was out of the bag.

Chapter 9

We assembled at six in the morning and bused uptown. Sam seemed rested and reflective. I was rested and jittery.

By six-thirty we were standing across the street from Joe Grablewski's place. We had no idea when he would emerge to begin his labors at Bookers.

At seven-thirty, two young women exited the dwelling. Then a substantial woman with a dog. Next, an old man with a cane.

"How are we going to get past the street door once he leaves?" I asked Sam nervously. "And what about the apartment door?"

It had dawned on me that despite Tully's bravado, he was hardly a seasoned burglar—as far as I knew. I wondered how thoroughly he had thought through this adventure.

Sam smiled. "I am prepared," he said simply, and went on to extract an ordinary brown shoelace from his pocket.

"What is that for?"

"Just watch," he said.

He walked quickly across the street and deftly placed the shoelace fully extended along the bottom of the outer door. Then he rejoined me.

"Now, when the door is opened, the shoelace slips down into the crack," he explained. "Nine times out of ten it keeps the door from engaging the lock again."

I wanted to ask him some questions about that strange homegrown shoelace procedure, but then Joseph Grablewski came into view. He was wearing exactly the same clothes he had worn before and was carrying what seemed to be his writing kit in a small plastic shopping bag.

Grablewski marched uptown toward Bookers, looking neither left nor right.

"Now?" I asked Tully.

"Now."

We hurried to the door. The shoelace trick had worked. The door was about a fifth of an inch ajar.

Once inside the hallway, we got an even bigger break: there was no trouble at all with the lobby door. That lock had been broken some time ago, by the look of it, and never repaired. The mailbox identified Grablewski's apartment as number 3D.

It was dark and quiet. There was the strong odor of commercial disinfectant and bug spray. The air of shabbiness was also heavy—in the cheap, worn hall carpets, in the faded wallpaper—but the building was relatively clean.

"I don't like this," I whispered.

"In for a penny, in for a pound," Tully retorted.

"No, Sam! This isn't my style. I don't want to smash doors down for any reason."

"Smash? What are you talking about? Easy does it. That's my style. I can get a door open so soft and gentle that even Pickles wouldn't know it was happening."

For some reason, I found that hard to believe.

"Look, honey, why don't you just stay right here? Make believe you're reading the mailboxes. Count to a hundred—slow—then just walk on up."

Panic? Dread? Guilt? I don't know what came over me at that moment, but I realized I couldn't go through with it.

"We're leaving now, Tully," I said.

"Are you crazy?"

"Now!" I almost shouted. I walked out. An angry Sam Tully followed me. I walked quickly. He was yelling in my ear: "What's the matter with you? We were already inside! There was nothing to be afraid of. We're not thieves."

I stopped and whirled to face him.

"No breaking and entering! Get it, Sam? Not now, not ever. So why don't you just calm down and come back downtown with me. I'll make you a cup of coffee."

"You keep changing plans so fast, Nestleton. How do I know you won't suddenly decide to throw me out of the cab on the way down?"

I didn't, of course. But I was tempted because he kept muttering "so close . . . so damn close."

"I don't like the way they're looking at me, honey."

"They" meant my cats.

"They just find you fascinating," I assured him.

"That gray one with the stump of a tail looks dangerous. I think he'd even give Pickles a run for his money."

"No, not at all. Pancho is a . . . a pussycat."

Tully grunted. "If you say so. Just let him keep his distance from me. And where's that coffee, Nestleton?"

I made instant coffee, the only kind I had on hand. He was sitting forlornly on the sofa.

I felt obliged to apologize. "I led you on a wild-goose chase, Sam. I'm sorry."

"It was our only shot, Nestleton. Now we're up against a brick wall. Or, to put it another way, there are no more breathing holes for us seals."

"No ends justify any means," I said.

"Hell, Nestleton, if you want to philosophize, let's go to a bar."

We didn't go to a bar and we didn't philosophize anymore. In fact, we both sank into a defeatist torpor: sipping coffee, watching the cats, watching the fan revolve.

From time to time Tully would burst out of his torpor with a comment like: "We were already inside the building. It would have been so easy." Then silence again.

Several times I started to tell him about seeing Pernell Jacobs, or seeing an apparition of him, but each time I stopped. The whole incident embarrassed me.

"Put on some music," Sam suggested.

"What kind would you like?"

"It don't matter as long as it's a lady singer."

I stood up and headed for my primitive music system.

"Wait, Nestleton! What the hell is that noise?"

"What noise?"

"Listen."

I did. It was one of my cats using something or other as his scratching board. They did that all the time. They wouldn't touch the real scratching board I got them from the pet store, but they happily ruined slipcovers and wicker laundry baskets. It was a losing battle trying to train them.

I looked for the culprit. It wasn't Bushy. He was snoozing on the floor.

It had to be Pancho. But he wasn't at the chair or the sofa, his usual scratching posts.

Then I spotted the felon. He was on the far side of the toy cat, scratching away. I walked over quickly and shoved him away. He was only able to abuse poor Dante in that way because Dante was wedged into the corner, making the wheels inoperable. I pulled the toy cat away from the wall.

"He really did a job on it," noted Sam.

Indeed, Pancho had shredded the mouton fur on one side.

"Look, Sam," I said. "It was padded with newspaper underneath."

"So?"

"That doesn't make sense in a well-made toy."

"Maybe it only looks well made."

I circled Dante warily, suspiciously.

"Did I tell you, Tully, that Mary had taped the exorbitant cat-sitting fee—the cash—under Dante's belly? The so-called cat-sitting fee, that is."

"Yeah, you said."

"I always thought *that* was the reason she lugged that stupid toy along with her."

"Maybe she was lonely."

I kept circling.

"You know what I'm thinking, Tully? That maybe there was a real reason for Dante."

"Like what?"

"A message in a bottle kind of thing."

"Come on, Nestleton. Mary was a sophisticated lady."

"Exactly. What better way to proceed? A method that no one would believe she'd employ. Least of all her murderer."

"Hold on. The heat has gotten to you, doll. Or maybe you can't handle a losing streak, which is what we're on. Are you really telling me that Mary put something important inside that goofy cat?"

"Yes, I believe she did."

"Give me a break, Nestleton."

"There's only one way to find out."

"That's for sure. But how about a little wager to pass the time?"

There was a hint of nastiness in his voice. Vengeance? His way to get back at me for aborting the break-in?

"A wager on what, Tully?" I asked.

"If there's something important inside that thing . . . if you find something having to do with the matters at hand . . . I'll buy you and your friends a blowout meal at that fancy Italian restaurant down on West Broadway, the one with the black pasta for twenty-two-ninety-five a dish."

"You mean Barlotti's?" I asked, eyeing the toy cat, hardly listening.

"Yeah, that's the one. And if the cat is as empty as your head has become, Nestleton, then you buy for me and my friends. Maybe even Pickles. He may like pasta. You game?"

"Sure."

Sam got up, kneeled by the cat, and anchored both ends of the toy with his hands.

I ripped away the shredded mouton.

It wasn't stuffed with newspapers. There was good wood beneath the fur.

But there was a single packet wrapped in a newspaper, and closed with tape.

I lay it carefully on the floor.

"Damn!" was all Sam could say.

I opened the packet with trembling hands. Inside was a stack of xeroxes. Some single sheets. Some multiple sheets stapled together.

I spread the sheets onto the floor next to Dante. Sam and I hunkered down.

He tapped one set of sheets and exhaled. "Will you look at that!"

I was equally astonished. It was a xerox reproduction of several pages from a Republic National Bank savings account.

The bankbook had obviously been laid open on the copier.

It was Joseph Grablewski's bankbook.

Sam let out a crazed-sounding laugh.

"Do you see what happened, doll? Mary beat us to the punch. She had the guts to break into his apartment. She had the same suspicions about Grablewski. Maybe she knew she was in danger. That's why she hid this stuff in the cat. And that's why she was bringing it to you."

"I didn't know the woman, Tully. But I doubt that she broke in."

"Okay. You got a point. Maybe she used different means. Maybe she just got friendly with the old drunk. Went to his place a few times. Played a little romantic game with him and all the while she was slipping stuff out, xeroxing it, and putting the original back."

"That makes sense. But Grablewski told me he didn't know Mary Singer."

"He lied."

"I guess he did."

Sam rocked a bit. "You suckered me into this bet, Nestleton. But I always pay up."

"Look at this, Tully," I said, tapping the paper. "He had only eleven dollars left in the account."

"Yeah. But look at all the activity. Lots of money in, lots of money out."

He was right. Grablewski had deposited money, left it in a few days, and then pulled it out. His deposits were all checks.

"Just enough time for the checks to clear," Sam noted.

The next sheaf of papers was startling. They were pay stubs.

Joseph Grablewski was receiving salary checks from the Star Market. Every two weeks. Different amounts for different numbers of hours worked—from five hundred to two thousand dollars.

And he was on the books. All the legitimate deductions were being made.

"This is impossible," I said. "Grablewski doesn't work in any market. He spends the day at Bookers, writing his play."

"He may not be slicing provolone at the Star Market, honey, but he sure as hell is washing their money. He deposits it, see. Then pulls it out and puts it somewhere else—in cash. Or he gives it to somebody. That's what probably happened to Mary's six thousand dollars."

The next xerox was peculiar. Mary had made a copy of a simple business card:

FAIRLIE RAWLS, CARPENTRY, it read.

She worked out of North Moore Street, in Tribeca. The slogan that ran along the bottom of the card read: "Specialty work from loft beds to rocking horses. Reasonable rates."

"What do you make of it?" Tully asked.

I held up my hand to signal that I needed just a minute. The carpentry business card had sent a jumble of disjointed thoughts pinging in my head. Like erratic hailstones. Rocking horses? A kid's toy. But what about Dante? Wasn't he a kid's toy also?

This lady carpenter could have produced him. If she could make a rocking horse, she could make Dante. I pointed to the poor thing, half his fur gone.

Sam was skeptical. He knew what I was postulating. He studied the card.

"Maybe," he said.

The next photocopied sheet was even more peculiar. Mary had xeroxed the back of a paperback book.

The title was not evident. In fact, the entire back cover consisted of a photo of the glaring author.

I was stunned.

"My God!" I yelled. "That's Grotowski. I had forgotten all about him."

"I thought you said his name was *Grablewski*," Sam chided. "What's the matter with you? Lost your memory?"

"No, no. Grotowski is someone else."

"Is he as crazy as he looks?"

I laughed. "Crazier. Joseph once told us in class that the American theater was about to be saved by two Poles. One a little nuts—he meant himself—and the other a certifiable lunatic—Grotowski."

I studied that face. Jerzy Grotowski had arrived in the U.S. from Poland and taken the theater world by storm in the late 1960s. He and his "poor theater." His theories were wild: The theater was doomed. It was all illusion and cliché. The actors had to destroy these illusions and clichés in order to create an authentic form. Get rid of props, lighting, scripts, and even audiences. He turned the Method inside-out, upside-down. One acted, according to Grotowski, first with the body. And the head had to be ready to receive dramatic truth from the body through wild exercises. The body informed the mind.

"Sam," I said, "a Grotowski production of a play was like nothing you have ever seen before. His actors walked on their hands, crawled, screamed. And they were often naked."

"Not my cup of tea," he replied.

I wondered what had happened to him and his theater and his theories. Was he dead?

Then I remembered reading once about one of his pet theories: The actor, he said, should approach his craft like the medieval wood-carver who tried to recreate in his block of wood a form that already existed in the wood itself.

I don't know why that popped into my head right

then, but it seemed relevant, important, somehow connecting to Dante and rocking horses and that carpenter.

The final xerox sheaf was three stapled pages. It was a list—some fifty names arranged alphabetically by last name.

All appeared to be women's names.

Then I saw the entry: Singer, Mary.

Sam had noticed it too. "Now we're cooking," he said dramatically.

"Yes. But what does it mean, Tully? Who are these people?"

Sam mused, "What do they have in common? Maybe they're all dead. Maybe they all live on Spring Street. Maybe they're all accountants."

"Maybe they don't have anything in common."

"They have to share something if they're on the same list. Lists are never random, honey."

There was only one way to deal with it. Sam took down the Manhattan telephone directory. I began reading off the names to him. Not surprisingly, only twelve out of the fifty names were represented in the Manhattan White Pages; and given that many people now use only their initials in telephone listings, we couldn't be sure of at least five of those twelve.

The other thirty-eight names represented people who either did not live in the city, or lived here but had unlisted numbers, or were, heaven forbid, dead.

"You start making the calls," Tully instructed me. "I have an ugly voice."

"What kind of approach do you suggest?"

"Go for the gold."

"What does that mean?"

"It means don't bother with a cover story. Get to the damn point right away. You're a friend of Mary Singer's. You need information about her life and death."

I didn't like his tone of voice. I said, a bit nastily, "Remember, you owe me a dinner at Barlotti's."

Pancho zoomed by just then. Tully flinched and followed Panch's progress out of the room. I picked up the phone and dialed the first of the dozen numbers.

That first call, and the three subsequent ones, were busts. I got an answering machine in all four cases. I simply stated I was a friend of Mary Singer's and needed to speak to the person about her. I left my home phone number on each person's tape.

On the fifth call, a woman answered. The moment she heard the name Mary Singer she hung up. Without saying a word. Just hung up.

Even odder, the next respondent, also a woman, did the same thing.

Number seven was not at home, and no answering machine kicked in.

When I reached number eight, Yvonne Bender, I identified myself once more as Mary's friend and asked if she had known Mary.

I heard the woman's sudden intake of breath. But she did not hang up. She didn't answer the question, but she didn't break the connection, either. It was a fear response, I realized, a kind of paralysis.

"Will you help me?" I asked.

No answer.

"You *did* know Mary, didn't you?" I pressed, trying not to sound accusing.

Finally she broke the silence. "Who are you?"

"My name is Alice."

"Alice what?"

"That doesn't matter, does it?"

"What makes you think I knew Mary Singer?"

"Both your names are on a list I have here in front of me."

"What kind of list?"

"Well, that is the problem, Miss Bender."

I heard dizzy laughter on the other end of the line. *"Problem?"* she repeated derisively. "Oh yes, it sounds as if you have a problem, all right, good Queen Alice."

"Did you know her or not, Miss Bender?" I asked sternly.

"Did you?" she challenged. "What was her middle initial?"

"I'm not sure," I mumbled.

"Did she wear white shoes in the summer?"

"Miss Bender, I can't see what any of that has to do with—"

"You claim to have been a friend, Alice in Wonderland. So how come you don't know what kind of shoes she wore?" More crazy laughter followed. "I'll tell you why!" She seemed on the brink of hysteria by then. "Because you don't know *anything*!"

"Miss Bender, please. Relax. Can we meet somewhere for lunch?"

"No. I'm leaving in ten minutes. For Tibet. The yaks are waiting for me there. They're throwing a tea party in my honor. But I'll tell you what I will do, Queen Alice. Before I depart I will deposit the recording of this conversation with the police. What do you think of that? You didn't know this was being recorded, did you, Alice the Genius . . . Witch Alice?"

I held the receiver away from my ear to escape her loud cackling. Even though she gave every indication of having gone off the deep end, it was important for me to try to remain rational and calm. "Look, Miss Bender, why don't we just—"

Slam!

She had at last broken the connection. I sat with the receiver in my hand for a few seconds, trying to take in what had just occurred. I couldn't.

I tried to reconstruct for Tully what had happened, tried to repeat verbatim her part of the conversation, but I had to give up. I think, however, I was able to give him enough of the flavor of it for him to understand the depths of her derangement.

He mulled it over in silence, then advised, "Keep on truckin', Nestleton."

I returned to the phone. But it was futile. The last few entries on the list either hung up at the mention of Mary Singer or did not answer the phone at all.

In a rage, I crumpled the paper and flung it across the room. Bushy pounced on it immediately and began playing a game for which only he knew the rules.

"Dammit, Tully. We seemed to be so close," I said.

"But no cigar."

"Everything we want to know has to be buried in that list. But it means nothing unless those people speak to us. Nothing at all." I laughed bitterly. "Without that, it might as well be the passenger list of the *Titanic*."

Sam got up and retrieved the list from the startled and much put out Bushy. He brought it back to the table and smoothed it out, then sat there staring at it.

"What are you looking at, Tully?"

"Just how pretty the damn thing is. All those names."

I fiddled with my coffee cup. Sam kept one eye on the list and one on Pancho, who was careening from window ledge to window ledge—which is why I usually open the windows from the top.

The frustration was beginning to wash over us, along with the late-morning heat. Is there anything more pathetic than investigators loaded with relevant facts but unable to make any sense of them?

"Well, look at it this way," Sam said.

"What way?"

"At least we know one thing about those women."

"We do?"

"Sure. We know they're plenty scared."

"Agreed," I said. "Do you want more coffee?"

"No thanks. But a bagel would be okay."

"None available, Tully."

"Life is hard sometimes."

"I think we have one more chance, Tully," I said after a minute.

"For bagels?"

"For breaking through."

"Speak, doll."

"Fairlie Rawls."

"That's a name on the list, right?"

"No. She's the carpenter. Remember?"

"Oh, right. But what does she have to do with anything?"

"I have a feeling."

Sam glared at the funny thing on skates for a long time before saying, "Why not! Give her a ring."

"Uh-uh. No more calls. We're going to take a stroll over there."

"Hey! Didn't that card say she was on North Moore?"

"Yes."

A look of delight had replaced his gloomy expression of a few minutes prior. "There's a great joint on that block—Walker's. How about that! We can have a burger and a couple of belts and *then* stroll over. I'll even pay. I might as well practice for that dinner I'm gonna buy everybody at Barlotti's. Yeah, I'll pay at Walker's, too."

"That's very generous of you."

"As Harry Bondo used to say, 'Quick with a buck, quick with a gun.' "

So there we were, at one in the afternoon: the dauntless, slightly felonious investigative team of Nestleton, Tully, and Bondo, seated at the old wood and brass bar of the tavern called Walker's. North Moore Street was in that section of Manhattan known as Tribeca—the *Tri*angle *Be*low *Ca*nal (Street)—which was in the process of a rapid and overwhelming transformation from forgotten manufacturing district, with the predictable sprinkling of pioneering artist lofts, to multimillion-dollar housing stock and glamorous restaurants.

Sam, in deference to the heat, was having his whiskey on the rocks, along with a blood-rare cheeseburger.

I ordered cranberry juice on ice and a small goat cheese salad.

Sam kept staring in fascination at the small disk of creamy cheese immured in the greens. "I can't believe this place serving something like that. Goat cheese! I can remember when they had bologna sandwiches."

"Everything changes, Tully," I reminded him. "This is a booming area now."

"Well, Nestleton, there's booming, and then there's goat cheese. They ain't death and taxes."

"No, I guess not."

He looked around with a kind of contented sigh. "Always liked this place, doll."

"Really? It doesn't appear to be anything special," I replied sourly. In fact, the greens were a bit—how shall I say—limp.

"But look at the walls. Check out those wood panels. I always had a weakness for wood panels."

What could I say? The man was enjoying himself. And he was buying.

When the lunch was over, we walked the block and a half to the address on the card.

It was one of those old factory buildings that had gone co-op during the 1980s. The loading dock in front was still there.

We clambered up to the building entrance. The bells were on the side of the door. Fairlie Rawls's bell was clearly marked. I pushed the buzzer and held it down for a count of three, then released it.

A voice came over the intercom: "Who is it?"

I called into the speaker: "We need to speak with you about your carpentry rates. We're renovating a loft."

We were buzzed in. The door opened onto a small bare concrete space. A wide industrial-type staircase fronted the space. We started up the stairs.

"No!" rang out.

We stopped in our tracks on the second step and looked up to the source of the command.

A woman was seated on the top step. On either side of her was a princely German shepherd dog.

"Hello," I said, trying to sound like Rebecca of Sunnybrook Farm, "are you Miss Fairlie Rawls?"

"That's my name."

"The carpenter."

"That's my profession."

Sam nudged me. I knew what he wanted: to end the charade.

"I'm afraid, Miss Rawls, we have gained entry under somewhat false pretenses."

A grim smile on her lips, she said slowly, "Is that so?"

She was a youngish woman, handsome, with a broad face and freckles. She wore a man's shirt over cutoff jeans. Her legs were long and muscular. The dogs, both of whom seemed highly intelligent and gentle, sat without moving. We felt no threat from them. Miss Rawls, however, was obviously wary of us. I didn't see how anybody could think Tully and I posed any danger. But, I thought, this *is* Manhattan.

"What I mean, Miss Rawls, is that I have a specialty job I'd like to speak to you about—but it isn't a loft renovation."

"What is it?"

"It has to do with toys."

"I do toys."

"Something like a rocking horse?"

"For a child, you mean."

"No. Not for a child. For myself. But not exactly a

rocking horse. I want something I can pull around. I want a horse on wooden wheels."

It was as though a curtain had been drawn across her expression. "A horse covered in fur," she said dully.

"Yes," I said. "In fact, that is what I want. That would be nice."

She brought her hands together in front of her face then. "I think you had better leave," she said quietly.

"But I need to—"

"Go now!" she commanded. "And take your friend with you."

It was time to go all the way. Now or never.

"I'm here about Mary Singer," I shouted. "And Joseph Grablewski. We found your business card in his apartment. Did you know Mary Singer? Did you do any work for her? Or for Grablewski? We're talking about murder, Miss Rawls."

She did not speak. She placed her hands on the stair, palms down, as if she were going to lift herself acrobatically.

Then she said something in a foreign language. One long, anguished word.

Neither Sam nor I had the chance to discuss translation. The dogs came rushing at us . . . hurtling down the steps like guided missiles.

We made a frantic break for the door.

I made it through, but Sam was only halfway out. They had his shoe.

"Pull!" he yelled. "Pull me out!"

The dogs were yipping and gurgling like hounds from hell. They ripped poor Tully's shoe away from his foot as he fell outside onto the loading dock.

I slammed the door shut.

"Let's get out of here, doll!"

Harry Bondo had never uttered a better piece of advice.

Twenty minutes later we sat, shaken, in a cut-rate shoe store on Canal Street. The sock on Tully's right foot was in shreds. No blood, though. He was lucky.

On the floor in front of us were three open boxes of new running shoes. Sneakers, as Sam referred to them. He had decided on a pair of those as temporary replacements.

The young Asian salesman who had delivered the shoes had moved off and was watching us with suspicion. Why shouldn't he? Sam Tully looked like a derelict anyway, and the missing shoe and dirty bandaged ear didn't help his image.

"Which pair do you like?"

"I don't know, Tully. How do you feel?"

He gave a big sigh, took off his other shoe, and began to put on a pair of red Converse high-tops. Once they were on, he just leaned back without lacing them.

"They fit," he said simply.

"How do you know unless you lace them up and walk around in them?"

"I know, honey. Just like I know it's time me and

Harry Bondo took charge of this investigation. It's getting too damn dangerous to let you keep running it."

"We did what had to be done," I countered.

"If you say so. But time's running out, Nestleton. We gotta hit the source . . . take the bull by the horns."

"I have no idea what you're talking about."

"I'm talking about Grablewski."

"What about him?"

"It's time to sweat that nut."

"Sweat him? You mean confront him?"

"No. I meant just what I said. Sweat him. Spook him. Make him run. I mean throw him into a panic . . . make it so hot for him, he'll run to the Man."

"And who is the Man?"

"It ain't him. He's in on it, but I think he's just a flunky."

"So why go for him?"

"Because he can open the door. We gotta make him try to run through that door."

"How?"

"I don't know."

He paid for the sneakers, and we walked out onto the sidewalk.

"You can always fry an egg on Canal Street in the summer," Sam noted.

Yes. It was hot. We strolled slowly, reflectively, trying to think of a way to spook Joseph Grablewski.

We passed an auto supply store. Inside the window were several posters of classic cars. One of them triggered a bittersweet memory.

"Look," I said, pointing to a Peugeot poster with the elegant lion that is the trademark of that company.

"You ever own a Peugeot?" asked Sam.

"No, but my ex-husband did. I did drive it, though. And I remember that the lion trademark was stamped on the ignition key."

"Right. All the cars do."

"Do what?"

"Put their logo on the ignition keys. Mustang's got a horse. Rolls has the two R's."

"And I remember there was also a small medallion on the key ring. There was a lion on that, too."

"Sure. Some people collect those."

I kept staring at that Peugeot lion in the window. But marital nostalgia faded fast. And in its place came a wild, beautiful scheme.

"Wait here for me, Tully. I'll be right out."

"Wait . . . where are you going? You don't have a car, honey."

I walked into the auto supply place and was back in five minutes.

"What are you up to, Nestleton?"

I opened my fist and revealed the object in my palm.

He stared at the key chain attached to a small medallion that was fastened onto a patch of leather.

On the medallion was a large "B." The letter was painted silver, or maybe it was just a silvery tin. The background leather was a soft brown.

" 'B' for Bentley," Sam hissed. "Wow, Nestleton. You are one sharp chick. How much?"

"Eleven ninety-five."

I let the chain dangle from my middle finger.

"It just might work, Sam. It would surely panic me if I was implicated. It would mean someone out there knows for sure that I was a major player in a capital crime."

"Yeah, now you're cooking. How are we going to get it to him?"

"He doesn't know you, Tully. Just walk past his table and drop it."

I jiggled the chain. "You think it's going to work?"

"Honey, what do we have to lose? As Harry Bondo used to say, 'Think like a honeybee, strike like a rattler.' "

The cab dropped us in front of Bookers. We peered into the coffee shop like hungry children at a bakery window.

Bookers was crowded that day. Grablewski was there, sure enough, scribbling. But he had been forced to share his table with two down-and-out, voluble thespians who seemed to be in the middle of a heated argument. No matter. Grablewski wrote on . . . cool, focused, self-contained.

For just a moment, a very brief moment, I had the feeling that all this was totally futile; that Sam and I were on a roller coaster to failure—all tracks leading to some fathomless wilderness.

We continued to watch. Grablewski stopped writing for a moment and closed his eyes to rest them. He now seemed a totally different man from the individual I had once adored in drama school. Different even from the man I had consulted a few short years ago when he was an ugly drunk. He was different in a way that had nothing to do with his sobriety.

What a long road this man has walked, I thought.

He went back to his play.

Sam said, "It's time, honey."

I handed him the key chain. He closed his fist over it and walked inside.

Yes, old Sam was really doing it right. He strolled into Bookers like a twenty-year denizen. He kept to the perimeter, going slowly, easily; a grizzled old actor with a heavy load of memories.

Then he cut to one of the aisles, moving faster, and just laid the key ring down on the table in front of Joseph, never breaking stride.

I kept my eye on Joseph Grablewski. He didn't seem to react at first. But then he closed his writing pad, put his pen down, and picked up the key ring.

Sam was back outside, beside me. "It's gonna work, honey. I feel it!"

Grablewski swung the chain methodically, slowly, back and forth in front of his eyes, as though trying to hypnotize himself. Finally he tucked it away inside his pocket. Then he did a totally unexpected thing:

he lay his head upon the table as if he had suddenly taken ill.

The collapse was short-lived. A minute later he stood, paid his bill, and walked out.

Sam and I averted our heads as he walked by us. He was moving quickly, heading uptown. At 55th Street, he turned west.

Grablewski was now walking at such a clip that Sam and I could scarcely keep up. But then he stopped abruptly at a pay phone between 9th and 10th avenues.

Tully and I halted in front of a small shop that sold nurses' uniforms. We could see Grablewski reflected in the store's display window. He stuffed a coin into the slot and dialed. But he never spoke into the receiver. Apparently the line was busy, or no one had picked up. He retrieved the coin from the return box and dialed again. Again, there seemed to be no answer. He slammed the phone down in a fury and took off, still going west.

He crossed 10th Avenue, walking toward 11th and the West Side Highway. But in the middle of the block he stopped and turned into a doorway. He fumbled for a key, found it, and opened a small, rusted iron door. Then he vanished inside it.

Sam and I approached the building slowly, walked past, and doubled back.

It was a very old, thick commercial edifice. The west wing of the building had a huge sliding door and had once, according to the yellowed sign still on the clouded plate glass window, housed an automotive transmission repair firm.

There were five bells on the side of the door Grablewski had entered, and a small neat sign identifying each tenant: two carting firms, a sheet metal fabricator, an import-export firm, an environmental testing lab.

We heard noises from inside.

"He's coming out!" Sam said urgently, pulling me away from the door and all the way across the street. We narrowly missed getting pulverized by a Department of Sanitation truck.

Indeed, it was Grablewski who emerged. He wasn't moving nearly as fast now. We trailed him to the corner of 11th Avenue, where he stood looking lost and confused.

"What the hell's the matter with him?" asked Tully.

When at last he made a move, it was to the nearest public phone. We watched while he made yet another call.

"We have to get into that building, Tully."

"I know. But how?"

"That shoelace trick of yours worked before."

"Nestleton, we're dealing with an industrial-type door here. It might not work. And he might not go back inside."

"But we've got to try," I insisted.

"This is a new pair of sneakers, Nestleton. Brand-new laces."

"For God's sake, Tully! This is an emergency. What's a lousy pair of laces at a time like this?"

Grumbling, he stripped a lace from one of the new sneakers, rushed across the street, planted it, and rushed back.

Then he smiled and said, "I thought you told me no breaking, no entering . . . not now, not ever. Yeah, I think those were your exact words."

"It's a derelict building, Tully. Can't you see that!"

Grablewski, across the way, was obviously still having trouble getting through to whomever it was he was phoning. He smashed the receiver down, re-dialed, *smashed*, redialed, and ended up kicking the post that held the phone up.

"I thought this character was an intellectual," Tully said in amusement, "a thinker, not a doer."

Grablewski finally gave up and walked back to the iron door, which he slammed shut behind him.

"Let's go, Tully," I said.

"Wait a bit," he said, restraining me. "Let's play it cool. It might be nothing."

"*No!* It has to be something. He's panicked and in a rage. He ran, didn't he? That's the den, Tully," I said, pointing at the building for emphasis.

"Den? What do you mean, like a bear or like a—"

"Never mind! Let's just go!"

"All right. Calm down. We're going."

As we snaked between trucks, I had the crazy urge to skip. I was reverting to childhood. Oh, well, it had been a long day.

Luck was still with us. The shoelace had worked again. The heavy old door swung open, and we slipped inside.

There were no lights on, but there was a cone of sunlight leaking from a skylight three stories up. Just enough to light our way.

We saw that there were no firms in operation in the building, no matter what it said on the bells outside. They were sheer fakery. The place was just a shell.

"What is this?" I whispered to Tully. "Airplane hangar? Mushroom cave?"

He shushed me and pointed to the far end of the space where there was a half-open door. Beyond it, a litter-strewn lot.

"He must be back there," Tully said. "I think I can see a shape."

We inched our way along the wall of that desolate, musty old building, toward the back door.

There were several alcoves along the wall with curtains made of ugly burlap. We pulled each one as we passed. They were either bathrooms or closets.

"A whole lot of johns," Sam noted in wonder.

The plumbing in each of the small rooms was fairly new. The storage closets were filled with paper supplies—towels, toilet paper, cups, and various kinds of soaps and detergents.

We heard loud snapping noises coming from the back lot into which Joseph Grablewski had vanished. When we reached the corner, we turned toward the back door, still keeping along the wall like tacking sailboats, Sam in front, me behind.

Suddenly he stopped, so abruptly that I banged into him.

"What is it?" I whispered.

"Roadblock ahead."

I peered around his shoulder. I saw a pile of mats stacked more than nine feet high.

"Walk around them, Tully," I urged.

"No, wait. Look at this." He pulled one mat out and dropped it onto the floor in front of me, like a welcoming mat.

I bent down close to the ground to examine the scratchy square.

Aut Caesar Aut Nihil, read the letters on the mat.

I had to suppress the cry threatening to break from my throat. Mary Singer's scruffy little rug!

Well, not the one from her apartment, but one just like it. And there were dozens more of them where this one came from.

We reached the partially open door and pushed it open a bit more. My nerves were like popping corn.

On the other side of the door, Grablewski had built a fire. He had used splintered wooden crates, piled up alarmingly high. Flames were licking at the afternoon air.

"What the hell is he doing with that bonfire in all this heat?" Sam said, no longer bothering to keep his voice down. "Toasting marshmallows?"

I shook my head. Aut Marshmallow Aut Nihil.

Then Grablewski came into view. He was carrying a small brown bundle, walking purposely toward the flames.

The bundle seemed to undulate in the haze of the fire. "It's alive, Sam!" I cried.

Grablewski walked faster and faster; he raised the bundle to the height of his shoulders.

"Jesus Lord! It's a baby!" Sam said.

"Stop him, Tully!" I screamed. "He's going to throw it on the fire! Stop him!"

We burst through the door together, screeching incoherently at the old man.

Grablewski turned, his face alive with fear.

Tully picked up a rotting burlap bag as he ran forward, then flung it over Grablewski's head.

I snatched the bundle from him as he stumbled and fell.

Now all was quiet except for the pop and sizzle of the flames.

"Is she . . . it . . . okay?" Sam yelled, breathing heavily and checking on the stunned Joseph Grablewski, who was woozily trying to regain his composure.

I looked at the bundle in my arms. It wasn't a she. But it wasn't a he, either. It wasn't a child of either gender. And it wasn't really alive. It was a mouton-covered toy cat—Dante's clone.

I looked up in wild confusion. My eyes caught a row of objects lined up on one side of the lot, ready to be conveyed to the funeral pyre. They were all toy felines on wooden wheels. Grablewski was dismantling them, apparently, so that they would burn faster.

I dropped the damn thing on the ground and rushed over to Grablewski. He raised his hands in fear, covered his face as if to protect it from a blow. Sam stayed close, but now proffered an old linen handkerchief to the man so that he might clean his face.

"We don't want to hurt you," I said desperately.

He did not respond.

"There is no one in the theater I respected more than you. Drunk or sober. You were the best teacher I ever had. But listen to me, Joseph: the law is going to crucify you. The owner of the Star Market killed Mary Singer. I saw him do it. And we know that you and Mary had a relationship. I don't know for how long or how intense it was. I don't even know the nature of it. But Mary was in your apartment. And she found and xeroxed key evidence. We have your bankbook, Joseph. And your pay stubs from the Star Market. You can't play this game any longer. We have proof that you've been laundering money for a criminal, Joseph—a murderer."

His answer was lost to me. His mouth had moved, but no words had come out. But then he seemed to regain some of his strength. "I had no idea they would kill anyone," he said.

"Who? Who do you mean, Joseph?"

"Pernell. And Flip. And Charlie Bright."

"Did you help them murder that woman?"

"No! I would never . . . All I did was collect money from the Star Market. And work here when they needed me."

"What work? What is this place?"

"A diet clinic."

"Cut the crap, you!" Sam shouted in derision. "You must think we're idiots!" And he moved threateningly toward Grablewski.

"I'm telling the truth!" Joe shouted back. "It's a place where women come to take off weight. They live here for weeks at a time. They wear almost nothing, go barefoot. They're allowed to eat one meal a day—meat and fruit. They're—given nothing but thin little mats to sleep on. And they pay thousands and thousands of dollars each week for the privilege. But it all works. They lose more weight than they ever thought possible."

It was an astonishing claim.

"And Pernell Jacobs ran this diet clinic?" I asked.

"Yes. Along with Flip Mariah and Charlie Bright. They were all in that play when Lara Streeter committed suicide. They realized what women would put themselves through to be thin . . . the extremes they'd go to. But it was Pernell who dreamed up the clinic program. He based it on Grotowski's method. You remember, don't you, Alice? I lectured on him at the Workshop. You were in the class. He said an actor is like a wood-carver. There is an ideal form already existing in the raw material before it is polluted by the clichés and illusions of theater. By the dead weight of it all.

"All the actor has to do is recover that ideal form—by using his body. That's how they built the diet program. It was crazy. All those fat women running about, pulling a toy on roller skates to remind them that they were wood-carvers. Pernell had them grunting and crawling like Grotowski's students did . . . to find the thin woman within. But it worked. Believe me, it worked.

"You must understand. These were women who were obese, most of them with eating disorders. They had all tried diets and spas. They were all depressed, some of them suicidal. Their obesity was crippling them. Pernell offered them a crazy kind of boot camp. They were literally incarcerated in this place. They began to believe—*Aut Caesar Aut Nihil.* And they *would* triumph. They *would* be thin. They would bring out the thin persona. Little food. Constant movement. A kooky spirituality. Yes, it worked."

"And this is the place where Mary Singer lost all her weight?"

"Yes."

"Why did they kill her?"

"They got greedy. They looked upon the women as no more than cash cows. Once they were in the program and losing weight—remember, these women had tried everything, without success—Pernell told them the clinic was in danger of being shut down. He told them he couldn't meet the bank payments and mortgage payments. They helped him out and kept helping. It was a lie, of course. Flip Mariah had bought this building for cash long ago, with money he made on some kind of ticket-scalping scheme."

"You're not answering me, Joseph. Why was Mary Singer killed?"

"She thought those requests for mortgage money from the women amounted to extortion. She had given her share, she said, and wasn't going to cough up anymore. She had begun to talk about the whole scheme with other people. She threatened to go see someone she had once read an article about. A cat-sitter who dabbled in criminal investigation. The so-called Cat Woman. You. So they killed her and videotaped the murder and gave it to the TV stations as a warning to the other women—to frighten them into silence."

"I knew that murder was staged for a purpose," Sam said.

"Yes," Joseph affirmed, "it was flamboyantly staged. Pernell rented the Bentley. They literally kidnaped Mary as she was on her way to see you. Charlie drove. Pernell had her in the back. He had on whiteface paint. You know Pernell. Ever the actor. It was a Brechtian touch, done to hinder any identification. And it worked, didn't it, Alice? You saw him, but you couldn't remember a damn thing. And Flip was waiting around the corner with his video camera, to show the world what happens when someone crosses their syndicate."

"Who were those women on the list?" I asked.

"What list?"

"The one Mary found in your apartment and copied."

"They went through the weight loss program at the same time Mary did. I was supposed to keep up the pressure on them, keep warning them that they would suffer the same fate as Mary if they didn't keep their mouths shut."

"When did the clinic close down?"

"The day after Mary Singer was murdered."

"Why did you get involved in this, Joseph? How could you?"

"You don't understand. Pernell Jacobs saved my life. I had been in a hundred drunk tanks and detox facilities. They didn't help. Pernell picked me up out of my own vomit because I had once been his teacher. He paid for my treatment at a famous hospital that specialized in treating alcoholics. I was kept sedated there. Pumped full of vitamins. They fed me the best diet in the world. They got me sober and gave me the strength to stay sober. I would have done anything Pernell wanted. I owed him my life."

"Where is he now, Joseph?"

"I don't know. Probably in New Haven. He bought a big old house up there last year. He said he'd always wanted to be able to throw firecrackers into the Yale Drama School from his bathroom window."

"Do you think Charlie Bright is there, too? And Flip?"

"Perhaps. I don't know."

"Did you know a diet doctor named Rodman?"

"No."

"Are you sure?"

"I have never heard that name."

It confirmed my belief that Mary's relationship with Rodman was coincidental to the case. He was just another thorn in her Calvary of obesity.

"Why were you going to burn everything?"

He pulled the Bentley key chain from his pocket and held it up then. "Was it you?"

Tully nodded.

"It frightened the hell out of me," Grablewski said. "I tried to call Pernell, but I couldn't get through to him. So I figured it was time to get rid of everything, to send it all up in smoke. I thought I'd be safe then."

"No, Joseph," I said, "you won't be safe. You're going to prison. The question is, for how long? I don't want you to die in prison, Joseph. Not when you didn't actually do any killing. So listen to me carefully.

"Sam and I are going to walk away from this thing now. You're going to go to the police—alone. Don't mention us or the medallion. Act as if you're walking in of your own free will. You have a story to tell. You have a confession to make. You'll set the record straight concerning the murder of Mary Singer. And you'll tell them about that house in New Haven."

He replied slowly, "I have no other option—do I?"

"No, you don't."

"I want you to know that Mary and I *were* lovers. But it was a brief, sad thing. And I had nothing to do with her murder. Believe me. Nothing."

Joseph stood up, wavered, steadied himself, then threw the medallion key ring into the fire. He began walking toward the door. We watched him until he had gone through it.

Sam looked utterly exhausted. I reached into his shirt pocket, found his pack of cigarettes, extracted one and placed it between his lips, then lit it for him.

"Thanks, honey."

"Just wait here for me, Tully," I said. "I'll only be a minute."

"Where are you going?"

I didn't tell him. A fury seemed to possess me. I began flinging the mouton toys into the fire, roller skates and all.

Chapter 10

There were five of us at the large table in the garden of Barlotti's: Sam, Lucille Petinos, Tony, Nora, and me.

As good as his word, Tully was paying off a gambling debt.

The moment I saw the menu I realized we had been thrust into yet another gambling situation. Would Sam have enough money to accommodate the eventual bill? It was a 50-50 proposition.

The thought of it made me a little testy.

It was three days after we had tracked Joseph Grablewski to that den of lunatic weight loss. It was twenty-four hours after the Connecticut State Police had surrounded Pernell Jacobs's house in New Haven and apprehended him.

Flip Mariah had slipped away. Charlie Bright had been wounded and captured in a shootout on the Connecticut Turnpike.

It should have been a celebratory dinner, but it wasn't. Other people at the table were out of sorts as well.

Nora, for one, was untypically reserved and quiet. She was probably still embarrassed by the disclosures about her past. Maybe she was afraid that I had told Tony. I hadn't, and didn't plan to.

Sam Tully's friend Lucille seemed distracted. She too said little. Maybe any separation from her Chow was just too much for her to bear. Or maybe she was just thinking about the doggie bag she would be presenting to him later that night.

But the real nastiness broke out between Sam Tully and Tony.

We had all ordered appetizers—everyone, that is, except Tully. He explained his abstinence by saying he was saving his taste buds for the octopus ink pasta.

Tony, who was drinking red wine, said to Sam, "It's too late for your taste buds as far as this meal is concerned, Pops. You started off with Wild Turkey." He pointed accusingly at Tully's empty glass.

Sam obviously did not appreciate being called Pops. He bristled.

"That's why people drink wine with their food," continued Basillio. "It enhances the food's taste. Drinking Wild Turkey before a meal is like painting your nose and tongue with shellac."

I cringed. Tony was looking for trouble. Was he jealous of Sam and all the time I had been spending with him?

But Sam seemed to take this provocation in stride. In fact, he just changed the subject completely. "I have decided to seek damages," he declared. "I'm in the process of interviewing lawyers."

"For what, Tully?" I asked, happy not to be talking about his whiskey consumption.

Tully pointed to his still bandaged ear. Then he pulled a piece of paper from his back pocket and held it up for all to see.

"What is that?" I demanded.

"This, doll, is an important document from an eminent scientist. A man who tells it like it is."

He shook the paper as if to rid it of impurities. Then he began to read:

" 'There is an easy and quite dependable way to determine what color eggs a hen will lay. If her earlobes are white she will lay white eggs. If on the other hand her earlobes are brown she will lay brown eggs.' "

He looked around, smiling triumphantly.

"So, Sam?"

"So, honey, this proves beyond a shadow of a doubt that earlobes are crucial; that the loss of one requires . . ."

He paused there for emphasis. Then he went on: ". . . a large monetary settlement. Cash, honey. Cash on the barrelhead."

"But Tully, who are you going to sue? You have no proof that Charlie Bright was the one who shot you. Besides, you're not a chicken. And you don't lay eggs of any color."

Sam dismissed my objections with a wave. He

folded the paper reverentially and returned it to his pocket.

Everything went well enough until the appetizers were finished and we were waiting for the main dishes.

Of course, Sam was a little soused by then, and agitated because he wasn't allowed to smoke. In addition, Tony conspicuously gritted his teeth every time Sam called one of us honey.

Suddenly, out of the blue, Tony asked Sam: "So, Pops, how's the book writing business these days?"

"Slow," answered Tully.

"Too bad," Tony said. "I know a guy who read your last book. What was the name of it again? Oh, yes. *Only the Demented Eat Ravioli.*"

Sam reacted angrily. "You got it wrong, buster. The title was *Only the Dead Wear Socks.*"

"Whatever. Anyway, this guy, an old friend of mine, really enjoyed it. He said it was very funny."

Sam's spine grew rigid. "Funny?"

"Yeah. He said he laughed so hard at your detective Moe Abscondo that his stomach hurt."

"Harry Bondo is the name of my detective," Tully snarled.

"Yeah, whatever. Anyway, he said you have to love any writer who steals from the Three Stooges."

Sam flung the half-loaf of delicious Italian bread at Basillio's head. It hit my true love on the nose. Tony flung his water glass, brimming with ice, at Sam. It missed. So he hurled the bud vase containing a white chrysanthemum. That missed Sam, too, but it hit a waitress in the rump.

Sam and Tony went for each other in earnest then. They knocked the table over in their tussling. Nora and Lucille were drenched with wine and ice water and rosemary-scented olive oil.

I remained unsullied.

When the smoke cleared, we were asked to leave the premises at once—no questions asked, no explanations given, no resistance proffered, no payment requested.

And so there we were, the five of us, standing on West Broadway, four of us in soiled garments. But oddly enough, the fight had cleared the air.

"Pops," Tony said warmly, "I'm going to buy you a drink."

Sam snorted. "Buster, I don't think you've got two nickels to rub together."

"You're right, actually," Tony admitted. "But we've got a rich friend." He put his arm around me and kissed me on the ear.

I knew beyond a shadow of a doubt that for the first time in a very long time I was going to get drunk. And I was looking forward to it.

As Harry Bondo might say, "If you name your cat Pickles, you'd better like vinegar."

Besides, hadn't that young waitress told me that every actress needed a company of players? Well, I had mine.

An Excerpt from
A Cat of One's Own

Chapter 1

It was the last day of November. Cold but sunny. A minute before the noon hour.

I was standing on Beekman Place—a very posh Manhattan neighborhood south of Sutton Place, north of the UN, and fronting the East River.

I was staring at a lovely row house.

The question to be posed was not, What is Alice Nestleton doing here, but What is Amanda Avery doing here?

I was on Beekman Place to see her. She had called me out of the blue. The last time I had seen or spoken to Amanda was almost five years ago, in Northampton, Massachusetts, where I had been involved in an ugly little episode with a group of classical musicians known as the Riverside String Quartet.

Amanda had helped me out then. When I saw her that last time she had just been fired from Smith College, where she had been teaching drama and literature while living a life of genteel poverty.

She was still absorbed in her never-ending critical work on Virginia Woolf and still trying to interest me in her never-finished one-woman play based on Woolf's diaries.

Now, Beekman Place?

She had obviously moved far and fast.

I rang the bell. She answered the door very quickly, as if she had been anxiously waiting for me. We laughed and embraced.

"You look wonderful, Alice," she said.

So, in fact, did she. Amanda was a small, strong-featured woman with close cropped gray hair. Her hair had turned irretrievably gray when she was in her early thirties and that suited her just fine. I'd never known her to have a man, a pet, or a vice. She was dressed now as she had always dressed in the past—like a Bohemian sculptor with a mile-long scarf and thick, vengeful sandals.

But the moment I entered that beautiful duplex apartment full of French country furniture, with windows on the river and on the street, I knew something had changed in Amanda's life.

Because I saw a dog.

It was an old Gordon setter bitch who didn't even get up—she just thumped her tail happily.

One rarely saw Gordon setters in the United States. They are bigger than their English cousins and much harder to keep in the average city apartment.

"That's Good Girl," said Amanda.

"Since when did you become a dog lover?" I asked.

"She really belongs to Ivan."

"Ivan?"

We sat down. Amanda served coffee and blueberry muffins and cleared up the puzzle: she had married a wealthy shoe manufacturer from Massachusetts two years ago. His name was Ivan Tasso. Six months ago he died suddenly from a blood clot on the brain. This, I then realized, was his apartment and Good Girl had been his dog.

"He was a rare man, Alice. Intelligent, passionate, funny. A kind of Don Quixote. But the only thing he could do right was produce shoes."

"Better that than tilting at windmills," I noted. I felt a bit awkward. It wasn't the kind of conversation I'd had with her in the past. We had never been intimate friends. We talked mostly about the theater.

"He did a lot for me, Alice," she said. "And now I want to do something for him."

I squirmed in my chair and sipped coffee from the oversize Provencal mug. What did she mean?

The man was dead. And why was she telling me this?

I changed the subject. "Have you been living here long, Amanda?"

"Two years."

"You're joking! You mean you've been in Manhattan for two years and you never gave me a ring till now?"

"I meant to, Alice. Really, I did. It was just that— well, there were some bad times. Oh, don't get me wrong. I loved Ivan and the marriage was wonderful. When I say things were bad I mean things were bad for me professionally. My project was going nowhere. I couldn't think anymore. I just . . . well, I began doing foolish things and—"

She stopped talking there, walked quickly over to me, and grasped my hands. "It is so good to see you again, dear." Amanda began pacing then, and talking very fast. "Ivan had a premonition that he was going to die, Alice. He asked me to do something for him after he was gone. He wanted me to get a friend for Good Girl. Because he knew she'd be lonely."

We both stared at the beautiful beast, who was still lying peacefully on the rug. Once again she thumped her tail. Good Girl kept her big soulful eyes trained on Amanda. The dog had that classic Gordon setter frame: rangy, gaunt, with large, tattered ears; her coat a soft black with creamy tan markings.

"When you say a 'friend,' Amanda, do you mean another setter?"

"No. A cat. Ivan made it clear I was to get a cat."

"But why?"

"Ivan's father was an onion farmer. He had a lot of house pets. As a puppy, Good Girl was raised with kittens. She loves them."

"Yes, that's quite common on farms," I said.

"Can you get one for me, Alice?"

"Oh, sure. I'll keep my ears open. I'll call you the minute I hear of a little one who needs a home."

"No!" she said vehemently.

It startled me. "What's the matter?"

"I want a cat now."

"Now?"

"Today. Immediately. I've procrastinated long enough—six months. I don't feel very comfortable with animals, Alice. I never have. But this is an obligation. This is something I *have* to do. Understand?"

"I suppose so, yes. Listen, Amanda. There's an animal shelter just ten blocks from here. It's called Abide. I could take you there and help you get a cat."

A little maliciously, I added, "After all, that's what cat sitters are for."

"Would you, Alice?"

"Of course."

She was hovering over my chair. "Where is this place? Shall I call a taxi?"

"Can I finish my coffee first?" I chided her.

She laughed. "Sorry, dear. Take your time." But

she was already clearing away the milk pitcher and brushing at the muffin crumbs.

I'd heard a lot about Abide. Many people I knew had adopted pets from that shelter.

But I had never been there and wasn't prepared for the reality of it. It was a large, busy, and efficient place, dazzlingly clean, where the staff was fiercely protective of its waif boarders.

Amanda and I walked into the reception area and were greeted by a young woman in a red smock. Soon the rather severe-looking interviewer appeared. She led Amanda to a corner spot where she grilled her unsparingly about her motives for adopting an animal. Presumably the aim was to weed out those would-be adopters who were sadistic maniacs, or not able to provide good homes because they were indigent themselves.

Only after Amanda passed muster were the two of us allowed to enter the feline domicile area.

The big cages inside the area were also spotless, and the tile floors and walls had been newly washed down. I caught a faint whiff of Lysol in the air. There were several open pens on the window side, where the cats were allowed to gambol either singly or in pairs, depending on their dispositions.

Three women volunteers in white-and-red checked smocks ran the show. A list of commands was printed in bold, block type on one wall:

DO NOT PICK UP ANY CAT WITHOUT PERMISSION!
DO NOT PUT YOUR FINGERS INTO ANY CAGE!
YOU MUST WASH YOUR HANDS AFTER HANDLING ANY CAT!

A smiling volunteer approached us. Her name tag identified her as Sis Norlich. "Just take your time, ladies. Look around. It's a full house today. Everybody here needs a good home. And aren't they all lovely!"

Amanda and I started making our rounds, Miss Norlich following us closely, as if perhaps we were not to be trusted.

And what a beautiful mélange of cats we saw. All shapes, colors, personalities. It was almost too sad to bear. If I had the room—say, a huge old house on a big piece of land with two barns—I would have taken them all.

I looked up to see Amanda pointing across the aisle.

There was a leg sticking far out of one of the cages. It was indeed a humorous sight. The cat attached to that leg was sleeping splayed out like a bear rug.

Amanda crossed the aisle and I followed her. The ever-watchful volunteer followed me.

We peered into the cage.

"Will you look at her!" Amanda exclaimed.

"Actually, it's a him," Miss Norlich corrected her.

Whatever it was, it was the strangest looking feline I had ever laid eyes on. The coloring of this cat was utterly unique.

"Black and tan," Amanda said in amazement. "Almost the same color as Good Girl."

I dropped my voice down to a whisper. "Did you by any chance tell the interviewer you have a dog at home?"

"No," she whispered back. "Why?"

"Sometimes cat people can be unyielding about canines. Better not say anything."

She nodded. "Have you ever seen a cat like this before?"

"Never," I said.

The small shorthaired cat had a two-color coat, perfectly bifurcated from the tip of his rosy pink nose right down the middle of his back, perfectly symmetrical. Tan, almost rust, on the right side, black on the left.

Perfectly symmetrical: even down to the ears, one tan and one black.

It was as if someone had taken half of one cat and joined it with half of another. He was a perfect little harlequin.

His tail, however, was solid black, and had a tuft of brown at the very tip.

"That's Jake. You don't want him."

It was a woman who had spoken, another volunteer.

"Why not?" I asked, catching only part of her name tag: Jill.

"Jake's something of a problem," she answered crisply.

I stared at the sleeping harlequin. He didn't look like a problem to me. But if a shelter volunteer was warning us off him, I figured it was probably best to heed her advice. I gently pulled Amanda away from the cage, and we resumed our walk around the room.

A black lady-cat with a white face caught Amanda's eye, as did a frisky tortoiseshell, and then a very young tabby with big ears.

Each one was taken out of its cage by a volunteer, and Amanda, following the hand-washing ritual, was allowed to hold him or her briefly. She had never held a cat before in her life, and didn't know what to do once the parcel was placed in her arms. I could read the fear on her face as each kitty mewled or nuzzled her or struggled to get away.

"All three of the ones you held are winners," said volunteer Sis. "It's hard to choose, isn't it?"

Amanda didn't answer. Instead, she suddenly wheeled and pointed to the cage with the harlequin cat—Jake.

"Him!" she pronounced loudly. "I want him!"

We were immediately surrounded by the volunteers, including a third woman, Ollie Something-or-other.

It was she who counseled: "We see by your interview report that this is your first cat. Believe me, Jake isn't for you. He's quite a handful."

"What does he do?" I inquired.

"He's just . . . difficult . . . at times," she stuttered.

"I don't care," Amanda declared stubbornly. "I want Jake."

"Just a minute, Amanda," I said. "Maybe you ought to listen to them."

She gave me a dirty look, her face set in stone. "I've made up my mind, Alice. It's Jake."

I said nothing further.

"Very well," Sis Norlich said doubtfully. "Go into the 'Get Acquainted Room' and we'll bring him in to you."

Amanda and I walked down the hall and, after washing her hands one last time, she went alone into a small enclosed space one wall of which was a window. A lone wooden chair was pulled up to the long, low table. The cat was delivered as promised.

I watched through the glass as Jake gave Amanda a lazy, appraising look, then promptly fell asleep again. Following his lead, she lay her head down close to his and closed her eyes.

Five minutes later one of the volunteers opened the door.

"We get along perfectly fine," said Amanda. "He's no problem at all."

Amanda took Jake out of the shelter in a new carrier. I toted the bag of litter, the litter box, and two kinds of cat food that Abide offered at prices below those of the neighborhood supermarkets.

We quickly found a cab.

"Maybe I ought to go back with you," I told Amanda. "Just in case."

"Just in case what?" she snapped.

"You know . . . what with the dog and all."

"How many times must I tell you, Alice? Ivan told me Good Girl was raised with cats, that she gets along better with them than with other dogs."

"I understand that," I said, "but you might need some help lugging all this stuff."

"Oh." She then apologized for snapping at me and agreed to let me help.

The taxi ride was fine. Being in a carrier in a fast moving vehicle didn't seem to faze Jake at all. In fact, he looked positively bored.

Once back in the apartment, with the carrier in the center of the living room, Amanda turned to me. "What do I do now?"

"Open it."

When she had done so, Jake stepped out, stretched, and began to survey his new home.

Good Girl, still on her rug, thumped her tail mightily in approval. Then she struggled to her feet and approached the cat.

Jake dropped low, belly on the carpet, his coat bristling. He began to hiss threateningly.

Good Girl stopped in her tracks, her feelings obviously hurt at Jake's out and out aggression. She walked back to her part of the room and lay down again.

I breathed easier. Then I showed Amanda how to set up the litter box and how much to feed the cat.

I was stunned when I noticed that Amanda was crying.

I rushed to her side. "What is it?"

"It's just that I realize the first wonderful thing I ever did for Ivan—I did after he died."

There wasn't much I could say.

In a minute she dried her eyes, thanked me for my assistance, and sent me away with three blueberry muffins.

That same evening, at home in my loft, I was recounting the events of the day to Tony Basillio, who had brought in a Turkish meal from a new take-out place on Bleecker Street.

He was eating as I talked. My two cats, Bushy and Pancho, were at our feet, trying to fake an interest in my story by sitting up attentively. Of course, what they were really doing was waiting to see if Tony would take pity on them and hand over some barbecued lamb.

When I finished the tale, Tony arched his thick eyebrows; the gesture only seemed to intensify his good looks. When he was younger, people said he should have been a soap opera hearthrob, rather than a penurious stage designer.

"Sounds like everything ended well, Swede," he

remarked. "The shelter placed the cat. This Jake found a cushy home for himself. Your friend Amanda made good on her dead husband's wish. The old dog has a new friend. And you did a good deed."

He chewed some, holding up his hand when I attempted to speak, which meant that his analysis was not yet concluded.

"The only thing I don't get," he continued, "is the cat itself. I mean, I just can't believe there's an animal that's one color on one side and another color on the other side."

"Tony, believe me, it's true. Think of a harlequin—or, you know, the jester in an Elizabethan drama. They often wore those pink and white costumes, the colors split right down the middle of the body . . . and different color bells on each shoe."

The ringing phone interrupted us. It was Amanda calling. She was frantic, almost screaming into the receiver. "Jake's in an absolute frenzy, Alice! I swear he's going crazy. He's in the litter box, and he's kicking every bit of the—the whatsit?—the gravel—out of the pan. It's everywhere I look, Alice—everywhere! He's acting as if he's lost his—"

"Amanda!" I barked. "Shut up for a minute!"

I had shocked her into silence. I could hear her breathing heavily.

"Listen to me, Amanda. I want you to calm down. It's nothing, what you're describing. A lot of cats kick their litter about as though they're digging a tunnel.

It means nothing. In fact it's good news. It simply shows that Jake took to the litter box quickly."

She didn't speak for a long time. Then she said sheepishly, "I'm a fool, Alice. Forgive me."

"Forget it. Everything's going to be fine. You can always call me if anything happens."

She hung up then. I began to clean up Tony's Turkish mess while he gave me one of his merciless reviews of the sets in an Australian tap-dance musical that he'd recently seen. I wasn't really listening. I'm an actress. Sets usually leave me cold. I prefer a bare stage, truth be told, and a good script—and an audience, of course.

The telephone rang again. Amanda, again. But this time she didn't sound hysterical, only worried.

"There's trouble, Alice."

"What trouble?"

"With Jake. He won't eat. Anything. I put out a bowl of dry food, like you told me, and a plate of that turkey in savory juices, and a bowl of water—just like you said. He walked over, sniffed at all of it, and walked away. So I tried giving him a dish of cream. No good. Even cottage cheese with peaches. He just won't touch any of it, Alice. He's going to starve if he goes on like this. And to make it worse, Good Girl is eating his food now. But he doesn't care at all! What am I going to do?"

"Amanda, it's nothing to get worked up about. Just stop worrying."

"How can I stop worrying? He'll starve!"

"Look, Jake's in a strange place, a new home. He may not eat until he feels comfortable. You have to remember, Jake isn't Good Girl. He may eat on schedule; he may not. He may eat only the dry food or only the canned, or both. You just can't predict what a cat will eat and when. They're finicky gourmands. Just put the food out and give him plenty of fresh water . . . and then forget about it. Look at my Pancho. There's only one thing he'd exert himself for, and that's saffron rice. You figure it out."

That crisis defused, Amanda rang off again.

Tony was on the floor now, playing his game with Pancho, whom he fondly referred to as "the psychopath," because Pancho spent most of his time fleeing or scheming against imaginary enemies.

The game was simple. Tony would meow, snarl, moan, growl, and make all manner of weird noises. Then, pretending to be Peter Lorre, he would inform Pancho that, no matter how long it took, he was going to "get him on some dark night and hang him high from a church steeple for his crimes against the feline nation."

Pancho, whom none of us would ever truly understand, seemed to find Tony's threats soothing. He sat about ten feet away from the sprawled out Basillio and looked upon him benignly.

Again the phone rang.

"Is that chick crazy?" Tony shouted. "It's only a cat!"

"Maybe it isn't Amanda this time," I suggested with a sigh.

Oh, but it was. Her voice, however, was far from hysteria. In fact, it was hushed and full of amazement.

"You won't believe what's happening now," she said, barely audible.

"Try me."

"I'm looking at Jake right now. Do you know where he is?"

"No."

"At the very top of the window. On *top* of the shutter."

"So?"

Her voice seemed to grow more and more desperate.

"How am I going to get him down from there, Alice? What if he falls? What'll I do?"

"Don't do anything. Cats climb. Cats jump. They get very high up sometimes. It looks scarier to us than it does to them. But believe me, he won't fall. He'll be okay, Amanda. He probably likes it up there. Maybe he wanted a deluxe river view."

I heard her short, disbelieving laugh.

"Take it easy, Amanda. Read a book. Listen to the radio or something. It might even be a good idea to get out of the house altogether. Why don't you go for a nice walk. Just forget about him for a while."

"I don't know, I don't know," she replied softly.

"He's just so . . . high up there. And the top of the shutter is so narrow. I'd hate to think of what—"

"Hey, Amanda. You ought to take a sleeping pill and go to bed," I said sternly.

To my surprise, she agreed. "Yes," she said, "I think that might be best."

Amanda hung up then. Tony looked worriedly at me. "We'd better get out of here, Nestleton. This Amanda is going to be calling all night. She's even worse than I was when you foisted those two Siamese on me last Christmas. Let Bushy answer the phone. Seems to me he's the one who'd know what to advise her about this Jake."

"What are you suggesting, Tony?"

"My apartment or a movie."

"A movie it is."

There were no further calls from Amanda for the next few days. On Sunday morning I slipped into a rather chic fall outfit, preparatory to meeting Tony. We would then proceed across town to the theater district, where my friend Nora ran a special little restaurant called the Pal Joey Bistro. Nora had only recently decided to start serving Sunday brunch, and Basillio and I had been invited for inaugural eggs Benedict and mimosas.

Just as I was leaving—and I do mean *just*—I was blowing a good-bye kiss to the cats while fishing keys from my purse—the telephone rang. Thinking it might be Tony, I picked up.

Alas, Amanda's whiskey-thick voice greeted me. All she said was, "Alice. He's gone."

"Gone? Who's gone?"

"Jake."

"What do you mean, Amanda?" I asked, trying not to sound annoyed.

"Just what I said. He vanished. When I got up this morning he was gone."

"Did you leave any of the windows or doors open?"

"No!"

"Then he isn't 'gone,' Amanda. He's only hiding. He's probably sleeping in a closet or behind a desk somewhere."

"No, he isn't. I checked. I've looked everywhere for him." Her voice had become tremulous.

"Don't be silly, Amanda. Cats can find all kinds of strange places to hide. He'll come out as soon as he gets hungry."

The dam broke then. She was crying inconsolably, muttering incoherently about her late husband; how her life had gone wrong and would never be good again.

I realized I'd better get over there.

"Just hang on, Amanda. Wait for me. I'll come and find Jake for you."

I called Tony and told him I'd meet him at Pal Joey, asking him to apologize to Nora for me because I'd be a little late.

Then I rushed out, hopped a cab, and sped to Amanda's place.

The man who answered her door was about forty, very thin, with a bushy mane of reddish hair. He was wearing a gray gym outfit.

"I'm a friend of Amanda's," he said in answer to my unspoken question. "Harvey Stith. I live just up the block. She called me. Sounded as if she was cracking up."

Harvey Stith! "*The* Harvey Stith?" I asked, shaking his proffered hand awkwardly.

"Well, I suppose so. I didn't think anyone remembered my name," he said shyly and chuckled.

He was wrong—*I* remembered his name. Stith had been one of those meteoric wunderkinds who exploded onto Broadway in the early 1980s. Singer, dancer, songwriter, director—you name it, he did it.

But then the bubble burst. I heard he had forsaken the commercial theater and accepted a position as director of one of those ambitious graduate programs in theater arts at a California university.

He ushered me in. Poor Amanda, the phone still in her lap, was on the rug beside Good Girl. Two more sorrowful creatures I had never seen.

I looked around the apartment, more critically this time. It had many nooks and crannies; many bookcases and shelves and cabinets and, obviously, many closets. Jake could be anywhere.

"Stay where you are, Amanda," I told her. "Harvey and I will find him. All you have to do is tell us which closets have trunks or cartons or hat boxes without a lid—that kind of stuff."

She pointed to the hallway.

"Jake-O!" I called. "Come out, come out wherever you are." I then commenced my search, opening the closet door. Inside were enough boxes for a flock of shy cats to hide in for a week.

Even with my head inside the closet, I could hear the telephone ring. I wondered if Amanda had made hysterical phone calls to everyone she knew, asking for their help in finding the cat. "Jake-O!" I continued to call. "You come out here this minute!"

It wasn't the cat whose shrill cry I heard. It was Amanda's—she was screaming into the receiver: "But how . . . *How*?! The banks are closed today!"

I walked quickly back to the living room and again looked to Harvey Stith for an answer. He only shrugged.

Amanda hung up abruptly.

She was on her feet by then, shaking, her face bloodless. "He said he has Jake," she announced in a monotone. "He said he wants $15,000 or I'll never see Jake again. He said he'd call back in twenty minutes."

"Is this some kind of joke, Amanda?" I asked.

She didn't answer. She knelt beside Good Girl and pulled at one of her ears.

"Something tells me it isn't a joke," Harvey Stith said.

"This man who called," I said, "do you know him, Amanda?"

She shook her head vehemently.

"Are you sure that's what he said? That he wanted $15,000 for Jake?"

"Fifteen thousand," she repeated. "If I want hm back. He'll call again in twenty minutes." And she began to giggle.

Oh Lord, I thought, she's going to lose control altogether. Harvey and I got her up and led her to a chair. She was tense as a trip wire, fighting panic.

"How could this person have gotten Jake?" she whispered. "How did he get in? When?"

"Call the police, Amanda," Harvey urged.

"No! No police! I want Jake back!"

"But this is insane. Fifteen thousand? You can't just give this man fifteen thousand dollars for an animal you've had for only a few days—a stray from a shelter."

Amanda looked up at me beseechingly. "What would you do, Alice?"

I couldn't answer. I didn't have $15,000. If someone kidnapped one of my cats and demanded a ransom for his safe return, I'd pay anything. But it wasn't for me to say what Amanda should do. The whole thing was so strange. More than just strange, it was unreal.

"Call the police, Amanda," Stith said again. "This is serious business."

"I said no!"

Harvey looked to me for support. But I steadfastly refused to intervene. There were conflicting theories about bringing the police in on kidnappings. Sometimes it worked out for the best; sometimes it ended in tragedy.

We waited in eerie silence.

The apartment became oppressive, as if it were sucking the air out of our lungs. Oddly enough, I could sense the presence of that harlequin cat.

The follow-up call came. Amanda picked up the receiver slowly and brought it to her ear. "Yes . . . Yes," she murmured, and then she fell silent, listening. She did not look at Harvey, or at me.

At last she hung up.

"All right. It's set," she told us.

"What's set?" asked Harvey.

"I will go to the bank tomorrow and get the fifteen thousand in twenties and fifties. I'll bring the money to 46th Street and 12th Avenue tomorrow night at ten-thirty. He'll turn Jake over to me, and I'll give him the money. I must come alone."

An expression of utter disgust crossed Harvey's face. "This is stupid and dangerous."

"Amanda," I said, "that is a very desolate area at night."

"I don't care. Will you help me—both of you?"

"How?" I asked.

"Just stay close. A block or two away. Then come and collect me and Jake. I know I'll be exhausted and frightened. I won't make it back home by myself."

What choice did we have? Harvey Stith and I made our arrangements: Meet at 10 P.M. at the luncheonette on 57th Street at 11th Avenue, then go and collect Amanda and, we hoped, Jake.

I went on to brunch at the restaurant. I didn't say a word about what was going on to Nora and Tony.

It was too difficult to explain—too—well, as I said, unreal.

I spent Monday in a fog of anxiety and indecision. For hours at a time I contemplated the possibility that someone might someday kidnap my own cats.

Several times I felt the urge to phone Amanda and tell her that Harvey Stith was right: the police should be brought in. But I never made that call. There are few things in my life I regret more than not making that call.

At nine that evening I took a bus uptown. Harvey was already at the luncheonette when I arrived. We sat glumly in a booth with ripped leather, drinking coffee, not talking at all.

There seemed to be nothing to say. Nothing about our common interest in the theater; nothing about each other's personal lives, nothing about Amanda; nothing about Jake the cat, the unfortunate kidnap victim; not even a banal exchange about the weather.

At twenty minutes past ten, we began walking toward 12th Avenue. The sky was like black velvet— that's how dark it was—and the wind off the water was cutting.

Once on the avenue, we turned south, heading for 46th Street, where Amanda was to meet with the kidnapper.

The piers loomed up on our right. There was not a living soul on the street. The only lights came from the truck traffic on the avenue.

At 50th Street, Harvey stopped and squinted at his watch. "We'd better hurry. The exchange should be happening about now," he said.

We picked up our pace, fighting the wind.

49th. 48th. 47th. No more words exchanged.

"I think I can see her!" he burst out suddenly. "Yes, I see her!"

"Where?" I asked excitedly, as we began to run.

"Up ahead, Alice. There! Thank God, she's all right."

Amen, I thought, seeing Amanda for myself then. She was leaning against a No Parking post. Waiting for us. And Jake was all right too, snuggled up against her.

Amanda must have seen us at just about the same moment, because she seemed to be smiling at us. She was waving to us with one hand and holding on tightly to Jake with the other.

Smiling, I said. But that wasn't true.

I was mistaken. That was no smile.

Amanda fell forward and, in that second, Jake leapt clear.

Harvey caught her. The dead weight of her body spun him around and they both went sprawling to the pavement.

Then and only then did I see the ice pick in Amanda's back.